Personal Liability of Public Officials in Virginia's Local Governments and Its Impact On Their Willingness to Serve

Personal Liability of Public Officials in Virginia's Local Governments and Its Impact On Their Willingness to Serve

George O'Neil Urquhart

WIPF & STOCK · Eugene, Oregon

PERSONAL LIABILITY OF PUBLIC OFFICIALS IN VIRGINIA'S
LOCAL GOVERNMENTS AND ITS WILLINGNESS TO SERVE

Wipf & Stock
An Imprint of Wipf and Stock Publishers
199 W. 8th Ave., Suite 3
Eugene, OR 97401

www.wipfandstock.com

PAPERBACK ISBN: 978-1-4982-3965-3
HARDCOVER ISBN: 978-1-4982-3967-7

Manufactured in the U.S.A.

Contents

Preface

THE TITLE OF MY thesis, as stated above, is primarily the result of a suggestion by Richard L. DeCair, Executive Director of the Virginia Municipal League. In the ensuing research on the subject of personal liability, the author has learned through informal conversations with several public officials in various local governments in Virginia that they are concerned about the threat of lawsuits and court action against them as a result of their actions as governmental decision makers. Many of these officials express concern that personal liability suits against them in their official positions could have an adverse effect on their willingness to continue in public office.

Recognizing that personal liability lawsuits against public officials are increasing and that the implications of this phenomenon are important in governing the activities in Virginia counties, cities, and towns, the author believes that an examination of public official liability, including an analysis of the impact of personal liability on Virginia local governmental officials in terms of their willingness to serve, is valuable to all state and local public officials and administrators in the effective continuance of local government.

Depending on the nature of the issue under consideration, a researcher undertaking substantial inquiry into that area tends to pick up much support along the way through to the completion of the planned search. This thesis has not been an exception.

Preface

First, I am grateful to Morton and Ruth C. Wallerstein who provided a grant for my study at the University of Virginia and to the directors of the Institute of Government at the University and the Virginia Municipal League who presented the award. I am also thankful to the directors of the Institute who allowed me the use of its facilities while in residence as the Wallerstein Fellowship Recipient during the 1977–1978 academic year.

The list of other contributors and supporters continues. I am grateful to Michaux H. Wilkerson, Assistant County Manager—Henrico (formerly with the Institute of Government); Francis McQ. Lawrence, Attorney at Law —George R. St. John Associates, Charlottesville; and various members of the staff at the Institute and the Virginia Municipal League who provided information and other assistance during the earlier stages of this research.

I am indebted to those officials of Albemarle, Chesterfield, and Henrico Counties and the City of Richmond, who allowed me valuable time to conduct interviews with each of them on this issue. Lawyers and attorneys from these localities and elsewhere who have been helpful include William L. Winbushe, Assistant City Attorney—Richmond; William G. Broaddus, Henrico County Attorney; and James B. Murray, Jr., Attorney at Law in Charlottesville. Reporters Robert Gibson of Charlottesville's *Daily Press* and Ms. Memory Porter have been tremendous assets by making available their newspaper files of information relative to liability suits in Virginia.

I am particularly grateful to my readers, H. Clifton McCleskey and Robert S. Montjoy, who helped me move this thesis along to its completion. Their wisdom and advice have made this research what it is and also have been comforting in that the anxiety associated with bringing this thesis to a close has been greatly reduced.

Finally, my wife is even more deserving of my love and attention now that she has spent probably more than her share of sleepless and lonesome nights while I was away at the University. I remain grateful to her for her love and support.

With respect to all of the above, I accept the sole responsibility of any errors as a result of selecting the material and choice of methods in presenting this thesis. I am equally responsible for material omissions which included could have made this effort more valuable.

July 1979 G.O.N.U.

Introduction

THE THREAT OF PERSONAL-LIABILITY of governmental officials resulting from their decisions and actions is of considerable concern to current office holders and appointed officials. Their decisions and actions are being challenged more often and more vigorously than previously noted by the community and the electorate in general; they are being drawn into court more often than before by civil suits that seek judicial relief from some legislative or administrative decision or act. Local legislators and other public officials are concerned about actions taken by the various state courts and the disposition of personal liability suits. Whether statutes, ordinances, or constitutions are broadly or narrowly interpreted and defined will determine to a large extent the legal limits of discretion and the acts of local public officials.

The primary intent of this legal analysis is to determine to what extent public officials as defined herein are personally liable for their official acts which injure others or infringe their rights protected under state and federal law. This analysis also should help provide the basis for a reassessment of state and local laws or policies which outline the official acts of local officials. The information necessary for this analysis was drawn from legal texts, court cases, law review articles, legal digests and personal interviews with public officials in four Virginia localities.

This paper is addressed to Virginia state and local legislators and executives at the local level. Both State and local officials have roles in correcting the dilemma which exists in the concept of personal liability versus the doctrine of official immunity. The State legislature has a responsibility to help clarify ambiguities in the law regarding these two conflicting or competing principles of the common law doctrine. There are at present no statutes which specifically address the issue of reconciling personal liability and official immunity, with respect to local legislators or chief executives.

The lack of uniform legislation throughout the State regarding privileges and immunities of local officials presents a problem for the courts when a ruling is being made on the question of immunity or liability of a local public official since judges must rely on a judicially-established official immunity concept as it evolved from the common law doctrine of sovereign immunity. The doctrine of sovereign immunity provides that "the king (state) can do no wrong" and thus, the state is a sovereign entity. The official immunity concept variously provides that judges, state legislators and to some extent, local legislators are absolutely immune for their official acts; they cannot be held liable for their acts carried out under the color of the law. This concept provides a degree of immunity for other public officials, for example, chief executives and local attorneys. The degree of immunity depends on the type of decision or act being made and by whom. The two types of decisions or acts discussed in the literature on this subject defy clearly-defined boundaries; "discretionary" decisions assume an element of judgment on the part of the official and a "ministerial" act is the execution of a function by instruction or without an element of personal judgment. To further complicate the issue a public official may commit either one or both acts simultaneously in the execution of a single function.

At the State level, legislators are absolutely immune from damages suffered by an injured or aggrieved individual. Local legislators are not accorded the same protection. Local legislators and chief executives may be granted "qualified" immunity by a determination of the court following a "good faith" defense. A section in this thesis will present an argument that where a local government is performing a "governmental" function, it and its officials should

Introduction

be absolutely immune from personal liability suits. In performing governmental functions local governments are carrying out the functions of the State, and therefore, should be extended the same degree of immunity afforded state officials. Judges are absolutely immune at all levels of government.

The rise in personal liability suits against public officials is in part attributed to the ambiguities and complexity in applying the judicially-established law. Part of the increase in such suits is relative, however, to the expansion of general education and knowledge of the law involving civil rights, the volume and type of private practice lawsuits involving doctors and lawyers, more active participation and reaction to the public policymaking process, a general erosion of faith and respect for the public office, and to the expansion of the role of government generally.

Lawsuits against public officials may also be attributed to several other related factors. People are generally better educated. Some are more knowledgeable of the basis and limits of political power and authority. Others have access to the legislative and executive decision-making processes and are more conscious of law in general. Citizens participate more fully and openly in the governmental process than ever before. More important, citizens are reacting more to government actions. Citizens, including those not affected by a particular decision or policy are not accepting official decisions against their individual interests as binding and final. Many are not content with exhausting administrative remedies before turning to the courts for a remedy. In bringing a suit to court an aggrieved individual may assume that there is a small chance of winning a particular personal liability suit against the public official. Nevertheless, at the urging of various organizations at odds with the government or the official and with a consenting lawyer, an aggrieved individual may bring suit merely to express displeasure with the activities of the official or the government. Another contributing factor appears to be the result of more indepth news coverage.[1] Such coverage of governmental-related

1. Interview with James B. Murray, Jr., Attorney,Richmond and Fishburne, Attorneys At Law, Charlottesville, Virginia, March 15 and June 30, 1978. Mr.

stories on a nationwide basis has influenced the actions and responses of individuals living in Virginia.

Perhaps a more profound influence affecting the increase in public official liability suits is the diminishing prestige and respect for most elected and appointed public officials and the public office in general. The general belief that governments' actions are more suspect than before has simultaneously contributed to a general erosion of trust in the local legislator and chief executive.[2] Not since the post-Civil War civil service reform era has this phenomenon been more pronounced than at present. In at least one respect the current problem of increasing liability suits confronting office holders is similar in substance to the claim civil service

---

Murray indicated that there is a "general increasing awareness of the ability to use the civil courts to get money," and in the process the "courts are. being misused"; lawyers are not acting to screen. cases before filing, and regrettably, some lawyers "encourage the filing of suit." Writing for the Urban Land Institute, the Stanford Environmental Law Society states in its article "Citizen Pressure, Power, and the Courts": "the mere threat of a suit can be an impressive political. tactic, expressing acute citizen displeasure with the activities of the incumbent government." See *Management and Control of Growth*. Edited by Randall W. Scott, David J. Brower and Dallas D. Miner (Washington, D.C.: The Urban Land Institute, 1975), p. 174.

2. One of the problems contributing to the rising incidence of liability suits involving public officials includes "the public's attitude toward municipalities." Today's citizens believe they can buck city hall. See Howard B. Camden and Richard J. Heskin, "A Look at the Crisis in Municipal Insurance", *Virginia Town and City*, Vol. 13 (January 1978) p. 12.

Kenneth Henning, another commentator on the subject, notes "there is a tendency among government officials to view (personal liability suits) and the accompanying damage awards against elected and appointed public officials as uniquely related to . . . the 'anti politician' reaction to the Watergate disclosures." See Henning, "Liability of Municipal Officials", *Virginia Town and City*, Vol. 11, No. 10 (October 1976) pp. S-9.

Following up on another article by Henning ("Public Official Liability: A Trending Toward Administrative Malpractice", *Report 8*, ICMA, January 1976), Nancy Mitchell Peterson writes: "Lawsuits are being used not to compensate citizens for personal or financial loss, but *to change the behavior of public officials*. Citizens seem to be using the lawsuit, instead of the ballot box, to hold public officials accountable for their job." (Emphasis original). See Mitchell, "Holding Public Office--A Risky Business", *Nations Cities* 14 (August 1976) p. 24.

reformers made during a period from approximately 1850 to 1883: that the public officials who are running our governments are incompetent. In addition to this claim citizens are currently concerned with the exercise and abuse of power in the wake of several scandalous developments in governments. Probably the most notable developments involving the abuse of power and influence are reflected at the federal level in the Watergate investigations, the Ellsberg Trial proceedings and more recently, the "Koreagate" deliberations.

No one would deny that citizens have always complained to some extent about a government's actions or inaction. They have complained about public official incompetence, inefficiency, unresponsiveness, lack of compassion or concern, and disorderliness. But with the exception of cases involving gross negligence on the part of a public official seldom were the courts involved.

This passing state of affairs suggests that traditionally, official decisions were accepted because of the general respect and trust in the public office and in the individual public official. This traditional acceptance of authority appears to have given way to a more inquisitive, indeed a more "rational" behavior on the part of most citizens.

Published information on recent court actions indicates that many suits arise also as a result of the decision maker's attempt to meet a public need that potentially affects the majority rather than a single or minority interest.[3] Of course, if the case is clearly an infringement of either interest, the burden of liability must be borne by the public official or the government.

In addition, it is conceivable that some personal liability lawsuits are the result of the official's beliefs or preconceived notions of the "proper" decision or the "right" action. Many decision makers are "purely self-interested" officials "motivated almost entirely by goals that benefit themselves rather than their bureaus or society as a whole".[4]

---

3. "The Accountable Society," 84–85.
4. Nigro, *Modern Public Administration 2nd Edition*, 176.

A final factor which affects the incidence of personal liability suits against public officials is that governments in Virginia generally may not be sued without their prior consent. This being the case, an individual may have to bring a suit against a legislator or chief executive even though the suit is not against the official, personally. These suits seek injunctive or declaratory relief. However, if in the process of an injunctive suit, for example, the local official is found to have acted negligently or maliciously, then he/she is personally liable to the plaintiff.

To reduce the incidence of liability suits against the public official and to remove the associated risks of holding public office require a. concerted effort on the part of the state legislature and local legislators. In alleviating the ambiguities in the law with respect to official immunity, the state legislature should move to adopt legislation which clearly defines the authority of local governments officials—in particular, with reference to "discretionary" and "ministerial" actions. Similarly, local governments should draft ordinances which do not invite misinterpretation by local officers or the courts. Whether statutes, ordinances, or constitutions are broadly or narrowly interpreted and defined will determine to a large extent the ability of public officials to continue with essential policy-making functions.

Public officials must become more concerned about the consequences of their public decision. They should seek adequate staff support which offers analytic advice on particular outcomes of decisions; become more familiar with the requirements of state and federal laws; consult legal counsel on substantive matters contained in policies; and, among other things, be fair and just with employees and citizens. Being diligent in these concerns will reduce the likelihood of a personal liability suit being won against the public official.

Personal liability lawsuits are permitted under common law doctrine. Under common law "public officials were routinely held personally liable for civil wrongs committed in the performance of their duties.[5] Also under common law the government was grant-

5. McManis, "Personal Liability of State Officials," 86.

ed immunity from lawsuits. In governments where this doctrine is continued citizens may bring a suit against the public official for a government action. This action is not to be construed as a personal liability suit but rather as a suit brought against a public official by an aggrieved citizen in pursuit of injunctive or declaratory relief.

On the surface, the purpose of personal liability suits brought against the public official by a citizen is to provide a channel through which damages resulting from a violation of an individual's rights pursuant to the protection afforded by the United States Constitution and other federal and state statutes may be recovered. The underlying rationale for the personal liability provision is to motivate public officials to be more responsible for their actions and thereby encourage them to be more careful and calculating in deciding public issues.

The concept of personal liability is a competing alternative to the concept of official immunity. Official immunity derives from the common law doctrine that if "the king can do no wrong," neither can his officers. With the ascension of William III and Mary II to the British throne in the late seventh the concept of official immunity gave way to the notion that public officials are no different from ordinary citizens when called upon to answer for an act which results in an injury to an individual. The royal edict by William III and Mary II provided that public officials could be called to answer for their official acts with the possibility of being held liable for negligence or malfeasance in the handling of public affairs.

The distinction between the acts of the king or state and his officers is explained by an analysis of the doctrine of sovereign immunity and the derivative concept of official immunity. Where the doctrine of sovereign immunity prevails the king (state) is not compelled to answer for its acts. However, the acts of the state are those acts done by its leading officials acting under the authority (color) of the state's laws. Thus, if the state is immune from liability, then so are many of its officials. This reasoning justified the creation of the judicially established official immunity concept.

A public official is one who holds a public office; a position "created by law with duties cast upon the incumbent which involve an exercise of some portion of sovereign power and in which the public is concerned, with duties continuing in their nature, and not merely occasional or intermittent."[6] One who merely performs duties required of him by a public officer or public agent, under contract, though his employment is in doing public work, is not himself a public officer or public agent, but a mere "employee" or in some instances an "independent contractor."[7, 8]

Whether a public official or employee is liable for certain acts is determined by the position held and degree of immunity protection. Legislators and judges are accorded the greatest degree of protection; executive officials and lower level employees are accorded lesser degrees. In addition to the position criteria, immunity from personal liability is determined by a finding that an official act involves personal discretion or is purely ministerial.

The dilemma inherent in public official liability claims is how to provide immunity for the public official and to compensate an injured plaintiff for damages suffered by an official's acts. The social objective is to find a balance between these two conflicting notions. The objective of official immunity is to provide the official with adequate protection against threats as a result of his/her public decisions—against harassment and frivolous lawsuits. The objective of personal liability is to permit the bringing of a suit against the public official by an aggrieved party so that, in the case of an intentional or deliberate violation of an individual's rights, such party may be compensated for damages suffered by the named official. Under the current situation in Virginia, if the public official is not found guilty of a violation, under certain conditions, no compensation is awarded.

6. *State v. Bond*, 94 W.Va. 255, 118 S.E. 276 (1923). For a listing of city and county officials, see *Virginia Governmental Officials* (Richmond, Va.: The Virginia Municipal League, 1971) and the *Directory of Virginia County Officials* (Charlottesville, Va.: Virginia Association of counties, 1974.

7. *State v. Bond*, 94 W.Va. 255, 118 S.E. 276 (1923).

8. For a discussion of personal liability of public employees, see Charles S. Rhyne, William S. Rhyne and Stephen P. Elmendorf, *Tort Liability and Immunity of Municipal Officials* (Washington, DC: National Institute of Municipal Law Officers, 1976), 286–306.

Introduction

Several alternatives may lessen the impact of personal liability suits against the public official and also meet the objective of the personal liability concept. Three policy alternatives are examined. Indemnification is the process whereby the government pays its officials for any cost they incur as a result of a liability suit against them. If and indemnification policy is adopted, the injured plaintiff could bring suit against the public official, and depending on the outcome, the injured plaintiff would be compensated by the official who in turn would be indemnified by the respective government. For examples of the application of this alternative, see cases, *State ex rel. Crow v. St. Louis*, 174 Mo. 125, 73 S.W. 623 (1903); *Roper v. Laurinburg*, 90 N.C. 427 (1884); and *Hotchkiss v. Plunket*, 60 Conn. 230, 22 A. 535 (1891). The second alternative would provide liability insurance coverage to governmental officials. Liability insurance varies by contract and insurer and is in some Virginia localities a form of indemnification. If this policy is adopted, the injured plaintiff could bring suit against the public official. Depending on liability and the nature and extent of damage, the court could award any amount of compensation to the injured plaintiff up to the amount of the insurance coverage.[9] The third alternative requires that the State abrogate some of its sovereignty. The provisions of this act could be stated so that the State would be liable for the official acts of its officers. Under this alternative, the city or commonwealth attorney would represent the respective government named in the suit. The injured plaintiff could be compensated by the government in an amount determined by the court. It should be noted, however, that not any of the alternatives provides absolute certainty that the injured party would receive compensation for damages suffered as a result of a government's policies or an official's acts or that the public official will be free of anguish.

The potential effects of personal liability on public officials are broad. With the exception of absolute immunity protection

9. For an analysis of the application of this alternative in Virginia, see Howard Dobbin's "Liability Insurance for Governmental.Officers and.Employees," *Virginia Town and City*, Vol. 11, No. 10 (October 1976) pp. 11–12.

granted. Judges, all alternatives noted above suggest that a public official may be asked to answer or explain his/her acts. If the official is not guilty under any circumstances, the mere nuisance of going to court may be sufficient to discourage many officials from continuing in public office.

Increasing personal liability suits against public officials—many challenging the officials' judgment—have significant implications for both the government and the official. As will be illustrated by several cases and examples, one of the implications is that many public officials may be less willing to continue to serve in their official capacities. A local case, *Fleming v. Albemarle County Board of Supervisors*, 577 F. 2d 236 (1978), serves as a good example for observing the impact of personal liability suits on local legislators and the respective government.

The Fleming case is the outgrowth of a controversial issue involving the rezoning of land parcels near the South Rivanna Reservoir which serves the City of Charlottesville and Albemarle County. Entered as a federal case under the Civil Rights Act of 1871 (42 U.S.C. Section 1983), Fleming sued the Board of Supervisors for $1 million to compensate him for the damages he suffered as a result of the Board's decision. According to Peter Bacque, reporting for the Charlottesville *Daily Progress*, the damage suit charged that the March 1975 Board of Supervisors had "discriminated against (Fleming) by refusing to issue a special permit for the 128-acre community near the polluted South Rivanna Reservoir because he is black." It is reported further by Bacque that "the April 1976 trial of that suit was foreshortened abruptly, when Judge James Turk, after hearing Fleming's side of the matter but only a part of the county's defense, told attorneys for the parties he believed a prior Board had settled with the developer."

In holding up the issuance of the special use permit, the Board which took office January 1976 was accused of "hankypanky" by the Judge. Judge Turk "warned (the Board) he would do all he could to see that the $1 million damages were paid out of their private pockets if it were the case that the Board of Supervisors

Introduction

had conspired against Fleming."[10] The foregoing brief points to two essential elements of this topic. One concerns the extent to which the Albemarle Board of Supervisors was able to continue with governmental and legislative functions for which its members were elected in the wake of Judge Turk's statement. The other implication of the suit points to the question of official immunity: how immune are local legislators to personal liability suits?[11]

Although I have found few cases other than *Fleming*, which might justify the threat of personal liability against public officials in Virginia,[12] the implications of this notion may be a mixed bless-

10. "Fleming Petitions Allowed", *Daily Progress*, June 15, 1978.

11. Interview with James E. Treakle, Jr., Assistant Commonwealth Attorney—Albemarle County, Charlottesville, Virginia, March 15, 1978. In the opinion of Mr. Treakle, writing to George R. St. John, Esquire, Albemarle County Attorney, the Board of Supervisors were barred from deciding the Fleming application because of a "statutory conflict of interest." Mr. Treakle notes that since the suit is "against the individual-named members of the Board and since the supervisors are not shielded by governmental immunity therein, the question is whether these supervisors possess a material financial interest (albeit a negative one), as contemplated under the statute." In his summary, Treakle stated:

> it is my opinion that each individual member of the Board must disclose his interest and disqualify him self from participating in consideration of the application which is the subject matter of the litigation. This disqualification is mandated by the statute because of the existence of the material financial interest.

James E. Treakle, Jr., to George R. St. John, Esquire, March 8, 1978.

On the other hand, questioning the Assistant Commonwealth Attorney's opinion on the immunity question, James B. Murray, Jr., a local attorney noted:

> The Supervisor Defendants are elected legislators and their action in twice denying the Plaintiff's application for a planned unit development was a legislative action. The law is clear that legislators are absolutely immune from a suit of this sort, *Tenny v Brandhove*, 341 U.S. 376 (1975); *Imbler v. Pachtman*, 424 U.S. 409, 47 1. Ed. 2d 128, 96 S. Ct. 984 (1976).

From an unpublished report supplied by Murray during an interview (March 15, 1978).

12. *Crabbe v. County School Board*, 209 Va. 356 (1968). Court held that a teacher's performance of a governmental function for his employer, the School Board, did not exempt him from liability for negligence; *Elder v. Holland*, 208 Va. 15 (1967). State police captain was held not immune from liability for

ing to those concerned about the quality of public policy-making in Virginia's local governments. On the one hand, decision makers may become more concerned and careful in their public and decision-making activities. On the other hand, if liability suits won against public officials become more widespread throughout the nation, the office of the public official in Virginia may become less attractive and rewarding. It may be, in the latter instance, that the most qualified persons will leave office after the first term or not seek such public office in the first place, leaving the office to be sought after by those who may be less qualified, and with possibly less to lose.

Local governments and many states are taking legislative action to lessen the impact of personal liability suits against their public officers. Many are providing some form of insurance for their officers, and a few states have limited or abrogated their immunity so that suits may be brought against the state or locality rather than against the official. A concluding chapter 5 entitled "Policy Recommendations For Legislative Action" provides a policy recommendation for legislation possibly to be introduced in the Virginia General Assembly during its 1980 Session. It is hoped that this study will be read and supported by either one or both the Senate Committee on Local Government or the House Committee on Counties, Cities and Towns and give support to the suggested legislation.

What is the likely result if no action is taken by the State or local governments with regard to personal liability of public officials? It is conceivable that public officials will be less willing to serve or continue to serve. Chester I. Barnard in *The Functions of the Executive* explains in his sections on "Theory of Formal Organization" and "The Economy of Incentives" that an individual will be willing to contribute his efforts to an organization if he recognizes net satisfactions. " The net satisfactions which induce a man

defamatory words spoken while performing his duties as State police officer; *Rives v. Bolling*, 180 Va. 124 (1942). Judgment affirmed against State policeman for his negligent acts in the performance of a ministerial duty. Note that none of these cases involves public officials as defined in this paper.

to contribute his efforts to an organization result from the positive advantages as against the disadvantages which are entailed" (p. 140). In another place in his book, Barnard states, in effect, that an individual's willingness to serve is the "net effect, first, of the inducements to do so in conjunction with the practically available net satisfactions afforded by alternatives" (p. 85). Barnard's theories help to explain and suggest that if there is not a net surplus of incentives for public officials, the State and the local governments should take action which increases positive satisfactions as against negative satisfactions.

There is no way to determine whether there is a surplus of incentives without identifying all of the incentives and disincentives and weighing each on the basis of responses by public officials. This task is outside the scope of this study. However, it is recognized that the threat of a personal liability suit may be only one of several disincentives against a host of satisfactions an official receives as a result of his/her serving in a public capacity. Returning to Barnard's assumptions, James Q. Wilson offers the theoretical perspective that

> the behavior of persons occupying organizational roles (leader, executive) is principally, though not uniquely, determined by the requirements of organizational maintenance and enhancement and that this maintenance, in turn, chiefly involves supplying tangible and intangible incentives to individuals in order that they will become, or remain, members and will perform certain tasks.[13]

13. Wilson defines "maintenance" and "incentives": Maintenance includes not only survival, but also securing essential contributions of effort and resources from members, managing an effective system of communications, and helping formulate purposes: In short, producing and sustaining cooperative effort (p. 30).

"Incentives" may be tangible or intangible and include any valued benefit, service, or opportunity in exchange for which an individual is willing to contribute time, effort, or resources to an organization. *Material incentives* are tangible rewards: money, or things and services readily priced in monetary terms. *Specific solidary incentives* are intangible rewards created by the act of association that can be given to, or withheld from, specific individuals. *Collective solidary incentives* are intangible rewards created by the act of associating

According to Barnard, willingness to serve is one of three "necessary and sufficient conditions" for the survival of the government.

The importance of the system of incentives to the effective continuance of local government can be drawn from Wilson's finding that "the higher a person's social class, as defined by income, education, or occupation, the more likely he is to join a voluntary association"[14] (p. 56). Wilson's theory may explain the behavior of public officials who serve in Virginia's local government:

> The upper-status person will naturally pick those (organizations) that enhance his status; at a minimum, he will avoid those that might jeopardize or reduce it. He may, of course, also join organizations offering material or purposive incentives; but he will ordinarily take care to avoid those that threaten his status (p. 61). The implication of this statement is brought closer home when we consider that nearly all local legislators in Virginia are volunteers; most serve on a part-time basis and do not earn their livelihood as a result of their membership.

The purpose of this paper is to determine the justification for and extent of the threat of personal liability suits affecting local government public officials. It is my contention, however, that the findings will indicate the thesis of this paper: That the increase in personal liability suits is a reflection of the complex nature of public decision-making, in meeting competing and sometimes conflicting needs and demands; and that such in crease, and therefore, threat of a personal liability suit against the public official

---

that must be enjoyed by a group if they are enjoyed by anyone. *Purposive incentives* are intangible rewards that derive from the sense of satisfaction of having contributed to the attainment of a worthwhile cause (31, 33–34). Wilson, *Political Organizations*, (New York: Basic Books, Inc., Publishers, 1973).

14. Wilson defines "association" as Barnard defines "organization"—"a system of consciously coordinated activities or forces of two or more persons" (Barnard, 73). Wilson defines the "voluntary" organization as an association whose "members are generally full-time employees and do not earn their livelihood as a result of their membership." (31).

will induce him/her to be more calculating in public decisions and actions.

Several judicial and legislative developments have been analyzed to support or refute the thesis of this research. Information obtained from various texts and periodicals have been supplemented by the results of an attitudinal survey (questionnaire) of selected public officials' responses to several questions and statements concerning public official liability and its effects. These sources, selected case studies and general opinion provide and form the foundation for the conclusion of this research.

The respondents to the questionnaire are elected legislative officers and chief executives from selected local governments in Virginia, each having a population approximately fifty thousand or greater based on July 1, 1976 "Provisional Estimates" provided by the Tayloe Murphy Institute of the University of Virginia. Fifty thousand is used as a starting point since it is expected that such localities have been exposed to the notion of personal liability of public officials. Jurisdictions with large populations (over 50,000) are more likely to have had a liability lawsuit against them or against their legislators and/or chief executives simply because of the greater number of people and differences of interests between groups of people residing in or seeking opportunities in the larger jurisdiction than in the smaller locality.

This research is presented in essentially five chapters. Following the Introduction, chapters 1 and 2 examine the growth of public official liability and the doctrine of sovereign immunity. Chapter 3 further elaborates on the legal foundations of personal liability with emphasis on the liability of the public official and impact of the Civil Rights Act of 1871 (42 U.S.C., Section 1983) on local governments and their officials. Chapter 4 analyzes three measures designed to alleviate the potential liability suits. This chapter also contains a case study of the localized effects of a potential personal liability suit against the Board of Supervisors, Albemarle County, Virginia. The results of the survey conducted in the four Virginia localities are also presented in chapter 4.

Introduction

Chapter 5 and the Conclusion summarize the point of the thesis and include recommendations and suggested actions. The recommendations are viewed as measures helpful to address the problem of official liability as it currently exists, and are therefore worthy, I hope, of consideration for adoption by both state and local government officials in Virginia.

I

Historical Development of Common Law Immunity and Liability

THE DEVELOPMENT OF THE concepts of official immunity and personal liability gives rise to two competing principles of the common law doctrine. The official immunity doctrine "for decades has shielded most municipal officials from personal liability for their public acts."[1] Public official liability developed from the notion that "no distinctions should be made between public officials and ordinary citizens when considering their answerability for tortious conduct."[2]

Although the principle of official immunity is the more it is important to consider the principle of liability for the relevance it has when considering its justifications and impact on the public official. In this respect, public officials are concerned about how these two principles may be viewed and balanced by the courts. It is reported "the judicial abrogation of the common law doctrine of official immunity by many state courts has stripped away the public official's immunity protection that was once thought to be

1. Charles S. Rhyne, William S. Rhyne and Stephen P. Elmendorf, *Tort Liability and Immunity Municipal Officials* (Washington, DC: National Institute of-1unicipa Law Officers, 1976) vii-viii.

2. Ibid., 1.

essential to the effective performance of his public duties."[3] "Much of the judicial confusion in the area of official immunity and liability has sprung from. the court's attempts at balancing the need to compensate a wronged plaintiff with the need to provide some form of security to an official in the performance of his duties."[4]

In connection with the need to balance and the need to achieve the advantages of both official immunity and public official liability, the public official and the courts have considered .the benefits to be derived by instituting the concept of indemnification. Although indemnification will be discussed later in chapter 4, it is important to note here that "with indemnification all of the 'benefits' achieved by the immunity doctrine can be secured without denying the injured plaintiff his day in court."[5]

Perhaps the earliest case on liability of public officials is the case of *Ashby v. White* 938 (1703), where Chief Justice Holt of England's King's Bench[6] propounded the notion "if public officers will infringe men's rights, they ought to pay greater damages than other men, to deter and hinder other officers from like offenses."[7] Justice Holt's ruling was based on a belief that public officials' conduct and the public service in general would be improved if a strict liability standard were laid down and, that in serving as an example, other officials would be inclined to be more careful in the execution of their daily public activities. Holding the official responsible under the concept of official liability would yield a greater benefit to the citizenry and society in general than by granting official immunity. Following Chief Justice Holt's ruling, Lord Mansfield, in the case of *Mostyn v. Fabrigas* 1 Comp. 161 (1744), expounded on the concept of official liability with a suggestion that a public official's

3. Ibid., p. vii.

4. Ibid., p. J.

5. Ibid., 13.

6. "Chief Justice of England": The presiding judge in the king's bench" division of the high court of justice,. . . See *Black's Law Dictionary* (St. Paul: West Publishing, Co. 1968.

7. Rhyne,·et al.,·*Tort· Liability and Immunity of Municipal Officials*, 1.

immunity should not protect the official in any wrongful conduct against the state or the people. Lord Mansfield stated:

> "Therefore, to lay down in an English court of justice such monstrous proposition, as that a governor, acting by virtue of letters patent under the great seal, is accountable only to God and his conscience, that he is absolutely despotic and can spoil, plunder, and affect his majesty's subjects, both in their liberty and property, with immunity, is a doctrine that cannot be maintained."[8]

Holding the public official immune from liability for his actions is as much a concern to local officials and courts of law as the concept of official liability. The concept of liability indicates that the official should be held liable for his acts so that. he would not use the power of his office illegally or abusively. Also by being more accountable for his act, the official would be more responsive to carrying out the letter of the law. The development of the immunity doctrine, on the other hand, supports the claim that public officials should be to some extent protected from the threat of suits in the line of their duties and functions of the office; that a certain amount of immunity is needed to allow the official to effectively perform his actions. It is reported:

> The reason given for this blanket immunity is not to protect corrupt officials but to free public officials generally from the fear of vexations suits and personal liability--either of which might dampen the ardor of all but the most resolute or irresponsible public officials in the discharge of their duties. Perhaps too, the grant of blanket immunity to judges and legislators implicitly recognizes that there are limits to the injuries which can be inflicted in the courtroom or on the floor of the legislature.[9]

On the development of the doctrine of immunity, another commentator has written:

8. Ibid., 2.

9. McManis, "Personal Liability of State Officials," 86.

> The doctrine was an attempt "to strike a balance between providing a remedy against public officials for tortious conduct and protecting public officials from unwarranted harassment and the inhibition that would arise if the courts passed judgment on the policy decision of a coequal branch of government."[10]

Immunity may be provided to local public officials in various degrees.. Complete or "blanket" immunity affords absolute protection from liability. Judges have enjoyed absolute immunity for many years. Some local, state and national officials have also enjoyed blanket immunity. "Qualified immunity "provides protection against ultimate personal liability and then only if litigation established that the decision was made in good faith, while absolute immunity protection, whether the officers acted in good faith or not, is provided against personal liability itself."[11]

The courts and various public officials have attempted to find a balance between the amount of immunity and the extent to which public officials should be held liable for their tortious conduct. In this attempt, the courts and the public officials have considered the alternative of holding the governing unit liable rather than the public official for the tortious conduct of its officials and employees. The concept of indemnification is believed to hold benefits for both the injured plaintiff and the public official. As will be discussed in chapter 4, local and state officials have responded with legislation to address the problem of official immunity from liability. Several states have adopted legislation which limits governmental immunity. The common law rule holds that the state is sovereign; it can do no wrong. However, the trend indicates that governments are becoming more receptive to the notion that the government should be liable for the acts of its public officials. One observer has written:

> Since 1950, the trend in the law governing the liability of public officials has been described as moving away from the official that is liable for his actions toward increased

10. Rhyne, et al, 3.
11. McManis, 87.

immunity for public officers and employees, and away from the position that the government· is immune from suit for actions of its officials toward increased liability of governmental units.[12]

The State of Virginia is immune from liability under the common law doctrine of sovereign immunity, therefore its public officials when acting legally and within the scope of their employment are immune from personal liability.[13] Legislative officials are absolutely immune from personal liability suits in tort actions.[14] Executive officials are usually accorded qualified immunity. The State of Virginia has not abrogated the doctrine of sovereign immunity. It holds to the common law defense that the State is not liable for the actions of its officials or employees. Virginia retains both state and local immunity, that is, like the State, local political subdivisions of the State may not be held liable for the·torts of its officials or employees.[15]

In its effort to find a balance between the conflicting concepts of the doctrine of official immunity and that of public official liability, the courts are finding that the concept of indemnification is a way to achieve the desirable objectives of both official immunity and official liability: to protect the zeal and efficiency of the public official by shielding him from liability and to compensate the wronged plaintiff by denying the tortious public official immunity protection.

Under indemnifcation the respective government "indemnifies" the public official against personal liability; the government pays any costs connected with the suit against him. It is reported

---

12. Ibid., 86.

13. *Elder v. Holland*, 208 Va. 15 (1967); *Sayers· V. Bullar,* 180 Va. 222, 22 S.E. 2d 9 (1942).

14. Ibid.

15. Committee on the Office of Attorney General, Immunity; The liability of Government and its officials. Raleigh, NC: National Association of Attorneys, 30. Also see Table 1, "State Decisions Limiting Sovereign Immunity" in this publication.

in the National Institute of Municipal Law Officers (NIMLO)Research Report 159:

> The purpose behind the notion of indemnification that has been developed by the courts and. Incorporated by state legislatures into various statutes is to eliminate the need for a broad application of the official immunity doctrine without sacrificing the protection that immunity granted the municipal official. Through indemnification official immunity is reduced in scope or even eliminated, thereby giving a wronged plaintiff a chance to prove his case against· a tortious.. municipal official and to receive compensation for his injury. The plaintiff is not denied his remedy, but neither is the efficiency or zeal of the municipal official reduced in any way. Through indemnification the municipality pays the bill for the official's misconduct. Indemnification eliminates the need for courts to maintain the balance between compensating the plaintiff and protecting the municipal official meeting both of these confliction social objectives.[16]

One observer has noted that the notion of indemnification does not respond to the justification of official immunity; that "while indemnification may relieve the financial inhibitions concerning the liability of public servants, it does not mitigate the deleterious and harassing effect of frivolous lawsuits."[17] Another perspective on the concept, however, indicates that indemnification may encourage more responsible official conduct. As noted, official immunity from liability is reduced in governments when indemnification is granted. Thus, the acts of the public official are more susceptible to public scrutiny. Also where the acts of the public official are not in the discharge of his official duties, courts have held that he/she may not be indemnified.[18] The courts have recognized that in order to punish the dishonest official, it would be necessary that all public officials be subject to the threat

16. Rhyne et al., 322.

17. Shortlidge, "Personal Liability of Local Public Officials, Part III and IV, 245.

18. Rhyne, et al., 324.

of liability.[19] In a landmark case, *Gregoire v. Biddle*, 177 F. d 579 (2d Cir. 1949),[20] Chief Judge Learned Hand justified public official immunity:

> It does indeed go without saying that an official, who is in fact guilty of using his powers to vent his spleen upon others, or for any other personal motive not connected with the public good, should not escape liability for the injuries he may so cause; and if it were possible in practice to confine such complaints to the guilty, it would be monstrous to deny recovery. The justification for doing so (denying recovery) is that it is impossible to know whether the claim is well founded until the case has been tried, and that to submit all officials, the innocent as well as the guilty, to the bother of a trial and to the inevitable danger of its outcome, would dampen the ardor of all but the most resolute, or the most irresponsible, in the unflinching dis charge of their duties. Again and again the public interest calls for action which may turn out to be founded on a mistake, in the face of which an official may later find himself hard put to satisfy a jury of his good faith. There must indeed be a means of punishing public officials who have been truant to their duties; but that is quite another matter from exposing such as have been honestly mistaken to suit by anyone who has suffered in a balance between the evils inevitable in either alternative. In this instance it has been thought in the end better to leave unredressed the wrongs done by dishonest officers than to subject those who try to their duty to the constant dread of retaliation.[21]

Until a remedy is found which is equitable to both the public official and the injured plaintiff or until a better "balance" between the two competing concepts is found, the doctrine of official immunity will continue to prevail in Virginia relative to the application and interpretation of the common law doctrine of sovereign immunity. In applying the official immunity doctrine, various

19. Ibid.

20. *Cert. denied,* 339 U.S. 949 (1950).

21. c177 F. 2d at 581.

degrees of immunity from personal liability will be accorded the local legislator and the chief executive depending on the scope of their decision-making activities.

II

Traditional Principles of the Doctrine of Official Immunity

THE APPLICATION OF THE doctrine of official immunity and the protection it affords public officials from liability depend on the nature of the decisions being made, that is, immunity from liability lawsuits depends on the extent *to* which a decision made by a public official is "discretionary" or merely "ministerial."[1] The courts' efforts to distinguish between an act of discretion and a ministerial act form the basis for examining the principles of official immunity. The first principle of the doctrine of official immunity provides that a public official be accorded blanket immunity or qualified immunity from damages incurred in the line of official duty. The second principle provides that a public official is liable for acts of misfeasance or negligence in the performance of duty where the decision is ministerial in nature or where the public official failed to act as authorized in a ministerial capacity.[2]

The courts have attempted to define the two principles and there by draw a distinction between a discretionary act and a

1. *Austin v. Richardson*, 1 Gratt. (42 Va.) 310 (1844); *Allen v. Com.*, 83 Va. 94, 1 S.E. 607 (1886); *Yates v. Ley* 121 Va. 265, 92 S.E. 837 (1917).

2. *Allen v. Com.*, 83 Va. 94, 1 S.E. 607 (1886); *Berry v. Hamman*, 203 Va. 596, 125 S.E. (2d) 851 (1962).

ministerial act. In one case, the distinction between the two acts was stated:

> Tort liability of a public officer to an individual-for his negligent acts or omissions in the discharge of an official duty depends altogether upon the nature of the duty to which the neglect is alleged. Where his duty is ministerial, he is liable in damages to anyone specially injured, either through nonfeasance or misfeasance. On the other hand, where his powers are discretionary, to be exerted or with held according to his own judgment as to what is necessary and proper, he is not liable to any private person for a neglect to exercise those powers, nor for the consequences of a lawful exercise of them where no corruption or malice can be imputed, and he keeps within the scope of his authority.[3]

Several definitions are offered for both "ministerial" and "discretionary" acts. At the very least a discretionary act includes "judicial acts, quasi-judicial acts and any other type of act 'administrative' or 'executive' are two terms frequently used) where some type of judgment or policy-making is involved."[4] A discretionary function has been defined as that function which is quasi-judicial in nature in that it requires personal deliberation and judgment.[5] A ministerial act requires a public official to respond to a given situation as programmed. A ministerial act is one which requires no decision or judgment but amounts only to the obedience of orders."[6] A court in Connecticut has remarked:

> The word "ministerial" under our law refers to a duty which is to be performed by an official "in a given state of facts in a prescribed manner, . . . without regard to or

3. *Doeg v. Cook*, 126 Cal. 213, 58 P. 707 (1899) and *Tomlinson v. Pierce*, 178 Cal. App. 2d. 112, 2 Cal. Rptr.700, 703 (1960) cited in Charles S. Rhyne et al., *Tort Liability and Immunity of Municipal Officials* (Washington, DC: National Institute of Municipal Law Officers, 1976), 15–16.

4. Ibid., 23.

5. Ibid., 16.

6. Ibid.

the exercise of his own judgment (or discretion) upon the property of the act being done . . . "[7]

In Virginia, the court has held that, generally, statutes which vest arbitrary discretion in public officials, without prescribing a uniform rule of action by which they shall be guided, are unconstitutional and void.[8] The court's decision is subject, however, to a qualification lay down a specific rule of action.[9] However, defined and distinguished, the line between what is discretionary and ministerial is not clear or distinct. For example, a public official may exercise both discretionary and ministerial powers. In a case on this problem, the court remarked:

> The main perplexity . . . is to determine where the ministerial . . . duties end and the discretion process begins. It would be difficult to conceive of any official act, no matter how directly ministerial, that did not admit of some discretion in the manner of its performance even if it involves only the driving of a nail.[10]

The doctrine of official immunity is an outgrowth of "judicial" immunity. As noted earlier in this research, judges have long enjoyed absolute protection from liability. When the official immunity doctrine was to officials whose duties were "not even remotely 'judicial' in character, then the courts classified these officials' acts as discretionary rather than judicial."[11] In order to invoke the protection of qualified immunity other public officials must establish that they acted in a quasi-judicial, judgmental, or discretionary capacity.[12] Absolute immunity mostly applies to public officials who are legislators or policy-makers. Qualified immu-

---

7. *Blake v. Mason*, 82 Conn. 324, 73 A. 7 2, 783 (1909) cited in Rhyne et al., 16.

8. *Gorieb v. Fox*, 145 Va. 554, 134 S.E. 914, A££. 274 u.s. 603 (1926).

9. Ibid.

10. *Ham v. County of Los Angeles*, 46 Cal. App. 148,189, 462, 468 (1920) cited in Rhyne et al., 17.

11. Rhyne et al., 22–23.

12. Henning, "Public Official Liability," 2.

nity applies to chief executives such as city managers and county administrators. Public officials are held responsible for their own acts in the abuse or transgression of their authority.[13]Public officers are not liable for the misconduct, negligence or omissions of their official subordinates in the performance of their. public functions.[14] This rule has been extended to the case of persons, such as contractors, consultants, etc. who act solely for the public benefit, though not strictly filling the character of officers or agents of the government.[15] Public officers are only liable if negligent themselves, or if they[16] cooperate in the wrong done. Where the duty of a public official is absolute, certain and imperative, involving merely the execution of a set task--that is, if the duty is simply ministerial—he is liable in damages to anyone specially injured either by his omitting to perform the task or duty, or by his performing it negligently or unskillfully.[17] For example, a public official may be held liable for defamatory words spoken while performing his duties.[18] When a public official has no jurisdiction over the subject matter, and when the act of which the complaint is made is maliciously or corruptly done, he is liable in damages *to* the party aggrieved by his conduct.[19] It is generally true that a public officer engaged in nonministerial—discretionary—duties will not be civilly liable for an act performed within the scope of his authority, even if that act is based upon an erroneous construction of law.[20] This rule is designed to protect public officers from the harassment of private individuals allegedly injured by the official acts, and *to* insure effective administration of the law.[21]

13. *Richhmond v. Long*, 17 Gratt. (58 Va.)375, 94 Am. Dec. 461 (1867).

14. Ibid.

15. *Sawyer v. Corse*, 17 Gratt (58 Va.) 230, 9 Dec. 445 (18 7).

16. *Tracy v. Cloyd*, 10 W. Va. 19 (1877).

17. *Wynn v. Grandy*, 170 Va. 590, 197 S.E. 527 (1938); *Berry v. Hamman*, 203 Va. 596, 125 S.E. (2d) 851 (1962).

18. *Elder v. Holland*, 208 Va. 15, 155 S.E. 2d 369

19. *Burch v. Hardwicke*, 30 Gratt. (71 Va.) 24 (1878).

20. *Michie's Jurisprudence*, 1974 Cumulative Supp.

21. *Bellamy v. Gates*, 214 Va.314, 200S.E. 2d 533.

Traditional Principles of the Doctrine of Official Immunity

In a 1975 case, *Wood v. Strickland*, 420 U.S. 308, under federal law, the United States Supreme Court appears to have added an additional requirement for granting by the courts of even qualified immunity, at least· insofar as civil rights are concerned. In addition to the requirements that the action taken be *discretionary* in nature rather than ministerial, and in good faith, the court held in this case that a school board member could not claim immunity:[22]

> . . . if he reasonably should have known that the action he took within his sphere of official responsibility would violate the constitutional rights of the student affected.[23]

> The general rule is that, in the absence of a statute providing liability, municipal officers acting in a legislative capacity are not liable in damages for their official acts, even though such acts are void as in excess of jurisdiction or other wise without authority of law. Likewise, no member of a municipal council can be held liable to any individual for the enactment or repeal of an ordinance within its authority whereby the latter has suffered damage.[24]

From the situations here presented, it may be seen that the courts have to look at and weigh several variables. The court must determine the hierarchial status of the official and the type of decision he/she is legally authorized to make. Since the same official may have a position where both discretionary and ministerial acts are within his/her powers, and since it must be determined at what point the act became discretionary, the courts have a somewhat difficult task. In this respect, court decisions on official immunity have become unpredictable.

22. Henning, 3.

23. Ibid.

24. *Shannon v. Hicks,* 434 F. Supp. 803 (1977); *Ross V. Gonzales,* 29 S.W. Zd 437 (Tex. Ct. Civ. App. 1930)—*Bricker v. Sims,* 195 Tenn. 361, 239 S.W. 2d 661 (1953); *McCray v. City of Lake Louisvllle,* 32. 7. 2d 837 (Ky. Ct. App. 960). · *Ross,· Bricker,* and *McCray* cited in Rhyne et al., 22.

III

The Legal Foundations
of Personal Liability

THE EXTENT TO WHICH public officials are held liable for their acts is based on the provisions of the various state statutes and constitutions and the United States Constitution. Case law and examples in the area of public official conduct are as varied on the subject of official liability as the several states. Virginia tort law is provided in statutes and case law. A remedy for any violation of an individual's constitutional rights by a public official is provided by federal statute, 42 U.S.C. Section 1983.

Personal Liability of Public Officials

In order to understand the notion of personal liability, a definition of the concept "Personal liability" is defined here in terms of "tort" liability. Several definitions have been given which define "tort(s)" from various perspectives.[1] Prosser defines tort as: " . . . a civil wrong, other than a breach. of contract, for which the court will provide a remedy in. the form of an action for damages."[2] He

1. See William L. Prosser, *The Law of Torts* (St.Paul, Minn.: West Publishing Co., 1971) pp. 1-2.

2. Ibid., 2.

follows by stating that this definition" . . . says nothing more than that a tort is one kind of legal wrong, for which the law will give a particular redress." Prosser recognizes that it is very difficult to define and make statements concerning a "tort." Torts can only be understood in terms of a broader context. Drawing from Prosser, one writer has noted that the best definition of the law of torts is " . . . a body of law which is directed toward the compensation of individuals rather than the public for losses which they have suffered in respect of all legally recognized interests . . . where the law considers that compensation is required."[3] A common thread in all torts is the notion of unreasonable interference within the interests of others.[4] Actions such as trespass, false imprisonment, assault and battery, inflicting mental distress, invasion of privacy, and negligence are examples of torts.[5] An intentional tort is defined as an act committed with the "intent to bring about a result which will invade the interests of another in a way that the law will not sanction."[6]

The acts of public officials may be questioned by any citizen affected thereby if he has suffered some character of prejudice for which.. he is entitled. to seek a redress in the courts.[7] However, an officer is entitled to the peculiar protection of the law in the performance of his official duties.[8] In Virginia, public officers duly equipped with the authority of the law represent the majesty of the law, and to them every citizen should yield prompt and willing obedience, and they should be accorded the fullest protection in the discharge of their duties.[9]

3. Brown, *Personal Liability of Public Officials*, 1.

4. Ibid.

5. Ibid.

6. See "Recent Decisions," "Civil Rights: Corporate Directors Held Personally Liable for Intentional Racial Discrimination Despite Due Diligence to Know the Law. *Tillman v. Wheaton-Haven Recreation Association*, 517 F. 5d. 1141 (4th Cir. 1975)" in 10 *University of Richmond Law Review* 197 (1975)at note 21.

7. *Gatewood v. Garrett*, 106 Va. 552, 56 S.E. 335. (1907).

8. *Mercer v. Com.*, 150 Va. 588, 142 S.E. 369 (1928).

9. *Hendricks v Com*, 163 Va. 1102, 178 S.E. 8. (1935)

Personal Liability Under the Civil Rights Act of 1871 (42 U.S.C. Section 1983)

Section 1983 of the Civil Rights Act of 1871 subjects all persons to liability for damages in cases where an injured party has been denied the protection of the fourteenth amendment of the United States Constitution at the hands of such person. Section 1983 states:

> Every person who, under color of any statute, ordinance, regulation, custom, or usage, of any territory, subjects, or causes to be subjected, any citizens of the United States or other person within the jurisdiction there of to the deprivation of any rights, privileges, or immunities secured by the Constitution and laws, shall be liable to the party injured in an action at law, suit in equity, or other proper proceeding for redress.

Pursuant to section five of the fourteenth amendment, Congress has the power to enforce this amendment "by appropriate legislation." Section 1983 does not establish new federal rights but rather creates a federal cause of action protecting already existing rights from violations by persons acting under the law.[1]

The provisions of Section 1983 did not apply to municipalities and counties until 1978, when the United States Supreme Court, in *Monell*,[2] concluded that municipalities are "persons" under the act. This ruling over-turned a previous Supreme Court decision,.. in *Monroe v Pape*,[3] that in a suit for money damages under section 1983 a municipal corporation is not a "person" within the meaning of the section.[4] Monroe was followed by *Moor v. County of Alameda*, 411 U.S. 693 (1973) in which the Supreme Court held that

---

1. Gary J. Spahn and David E. Boone, "Private Discrimination Actions Filed in Federal Court: Non-substantive Matters Affecting Liability and Relief" 12 *University of Richmond Law Review* 101 (Fall 1977).

2. *Monell et al. v. City of New York, et al.*, 436 U.S. 658, 98 S.Ct. 2018, 56 L.d 611 (Decided June 6, 1978).

3. 365 U.S. 167 (1961).

4. Spahn and Boone, 102.

"counties, like municipalities, are 'nonpersons' within the meaning of section 1983."[5] The Supreme Court also held in *City of Kenosha v. Bruno*, 412 U.S. 507 (1973) that a municipality is not a "person" within the meaning of the statute in both damage and equitable actions.[6]

When municipalities and counties are excluded from liability under section 1983 this increases the probability of suits against public officials in their official capacity. Although the suits are not against the official, in his/her authorized and official capacity, but, rather, against a government's practice or an erroneously constructed ordinance or statute, the imposition of such suit and the ordeal which follow could have a profound effect on the official: An injured plaintiff "may recover damages from the responsible official sued in his individual capacity, providing plaintiff establishes that the defendant acted in bad faith in performing his official duties . . . [7] In regard to "bad faith" in performing official duties, the United States Supreme Court held in *Wood v. Strickland*, 420 U.S. 308, 321–322 (1975):

> That the official must not only be acting in good faith, "with a belief that he is doing right", but also his actions cannot be justified by ignorance of "selected, undisputable law". Accordingly, if the official knew or reasonably should have known that his actions would violate a person's constitutional rights, he should not be immune from 1983 liability.[8]

A good faith defense is often difficult for the plaintiff to overcome. If bad faith cannot be determined,

> "then the suit is barred, not because it is a suit against an officer of the government, but because it is, in substance, a suit against the government over which the court, in view of a State's Eleventh Amendment immunity under the United States Constitution, in the absence of consent,

5. Ibid.
6. Ibid., 102–103.
7. Ibid., 104.
8. Ibid., 106 at note 82.

has no jurisdiction. In the absence of some statutory waiver, sovereign immunity bars any private suit seeking relief against the government.[9]

Although section 1983 covers a wide spectrum for redressing and protecting all individuals' fourteenth amendment rights, the public official who executes his/her duties with "diligence and fidelity" should not fear its coverage. In *Tenny v. Brandhove*, 341 U.S. 369 (1951), the Supreme Court held that legislators are immune so long as actions of the legislator are "fairly within" the legislative province.[10] For executive officials, the situation is not so clear: their acts are both discretionary and ministerial. For both legislators and chief executives, it is important to note that the Supreme Court held that section 1983 does not require a showing of a specific intent to deprive a person of a federal right, the mere deprivation is itself a violation.

---

9. Mashaw and Merrill, *The American Public Law System*, 659, 661.

10. Henning, "Public Official Liability, 4.

IV

The Potential Effects
of Personal Liability Suits

PUBLIC OFFICIALS ARE CONCERNED about official liability suits. Legislation dealing with the doctrines of official immunity and sovereign immunity is being hammered out across the nation. This concern and related activities on the part of the public official is one of the several possible indicators that the threat or notion of liability suits does have some effects.

The extent to which the effects of personal liability suits change the willingness of the public official to serve in a public capacity is not fully known. The only measurable indicator available at this time on the effects of liability is the amount and substance of legislative and judicial activity occurring in the states. Later in this chapter a case study will be analyzed to illustrate some of the potential effects a personal liability suit may have on local governments and their officials.

Several states are attempting to deal with the confusion which surrounds the competing, and in some cases, conflicting concepts of official immunity and the liability of public officials. These two concepts have some socially desirable objectives that should be achieved. The question in most liability suits is how much official immunity should be sacrificed so that injured parties can be compensated. This is a perennial question for many state courts and legislators.

States which are approaching the subject of personal liability have different views and opinions on the question of immunity from claims of errors and omissions in the performance of official activities. For example, in New Mexico, the legislature passed legislation which granted general tort immunity to local governments and their employees.[1] Additional information reported by the *Municipal Yearbook* reveal that:[2]

> In Arkansas, liability of public officials for misconduct of public employees has been limited to financial matters. only;
>
> In Minnesota, liability limits applicable to cities have been extended to include all city personnel. Previously, there was no limit on the personal liability of elected officials and department heads. The present law sets limits at $300,000 for a city and $100,000 for an individual; and
>
> In Oklahoma, governing boards of cities and towns are now required to provide legal assistance to municipal employees against whom a civil action is brought in relation to the performance of their duties. The municipalities, however, are not authorized to pay any monetary damages.

The Oklahoma legislature tort liability law affecting all local governments in that state and individual employee[3] the substance of the legislation is that the Act "abolishes the distinction between governmental and. proprietary functions (and provides that), generally, discretionary functions, such as legislative and judicial acts, and losses resulting from natural causes are exempt from suit.[4]

The Oklahoma law further provides that governmental employees are not liable unless fraud, corruption or malice exists. In contrast to the law as it existed at the time it was reported in the

1. *The Municipal Yearbook*, 54.
2. Ibid., 55–61.
3. Morgan, "Oklahoma Enacts Changes," 324.
4. Ibid.

Municipal Yearbook,[5] local governments are now "required to defend and pay claim if an employee or officer is found in violation of federal civil rights laws while acting in good faith"; however, no damages are permitted.[6]

It is also noted in the *Yearbook* that some states and, in some cases for special exceptions, local governments are required by law to carry liability insurance[7] on their employees. In such cases, however, it should be known that governmental and official immunity may be reduced, if not terminated, by the courts if liability insurance is available.[8] Although liability insurance will be discussed in a later section, it should be noted at this point that liability insurance coverage may not be available to many local governments because the cost of premiums have become prohibitive. Municipal and public official liability have become so noticeable in recent years that "insurers are either raising prices at astronomical rates or are deserting the market."[9]

Of the legislative activity dealing with official immunity, indemnification of public officials, and sovereign immunity, the two most comprehensive tort immunity statutes are the California Tort Claims Act and the Illinois Local Government and Governmental Employees Tort Immunity Act.[10] According *to* the National Institute of Municipal Law Officers (NIMLO) Research Report 159 (1976), the State of California Supreme Court struck down the common law of sovereign immunity that State and its political subdivisions previously enjoyed, causing the California legislature *to* adopt legislation which provided some liability protection for its local governments and their officials. The potential effects of

---

5. See text accompanying note 2 *supra.*

6. Morgan.

7. *The Municipal Yearbook.*

8. See Dobbins, "Liability Insurance for Governmental Officers and Employees," 11–12.

9. National League of Cities, *The New World of Municipal Liability,* 1.

10. For a brief summary of the provisions of the Acts, see Charles, S. Rhyne, William S. Rhyne and Stephen P. Elmendorf, *Tort liability and Immunity of Municipal Officials,* 287–307.

personal liability suits have been made more or less prevalent as a result of judicial and legislative activity in the area of municipal and official liability. Kenneth Culp Davis has written extensively on the subject, highlighting several important developments which have occurred within the last twenty years. Many of these developments are judicial in nature.

According to Davis, as of 1970, eighteen state courts had abolished "chunks of sovereign immunity by judicial actions."[11] "During the 1970–75 period, ten more state courts had abrogated large portions of sovereign immunity . . ."[12] In a November 1976 report prepared by the Committee on the Office of Attorney General, State decisions limiting sovereign immunity included Alabama: Jackson v. Florence, 320 So. 2d. 68, 74 (1975); Alaska: City of Fairbanks v. Schaible, 375 P. 2d 201 (Alaska, 196); Arizona: Stone v. Arizona Highway Commission, 93 Ariz.[13]

11. Davis, *Administrative Law of the Seventies*, 551.

12. Ibid.

13. 384, 381 P. 2d 107 (1963) and *State v. Stone*, 104 Ariz. 339 452 P. 2d, 513 (1969); California: *Muskopf v. Corning Hospital* 55 Cal. 2d 211, 11 Cal. Rptr. 89, 359 P.d 457 (1961); Colorado: *Evans v. Board of Courts Commissioners*, 174 Colo. 97, 482 P. 2d 968 (1971); *District of Columbia: Spencer v. General Hospital of District of Columbia*, 138 U.S. App. D.C. 48, 425 F. 2d 479 (1969); Florida: *Hargrove v. Town of Cocoa Beach*, 96 s 2d 130 (Fla. 1957; Idaho: *Smith v. State*, Idaho 795, 473, PP. 2d 933 (1970); Illinois: *Melitor v. Kaneland Community, Unit District No. 302*, 18 Ill. 2d 11, 163 N.E. 2d 89 1959); Indiana: *Campbell v. State*, 284 N.E. 2d 733 Ind. (1972), *Klepinger Board of Commissioners*, 143. Ind. App. 155, 2 9 N.E. 2d 160 (1968) and *Brinkman v. City of Indianapolis*, 141 Ind. App. 622, 231 N.E. 2d 169 (19 7); Kansas: *Carroll v. Kittle*, 203 Kan. 841, 457. P. 2d 21 (1969) and *Brown v. Wichita State University*, 550 P. 2d 66, 83 (Kan. 1975); Kentucky: *Haney v. City of Lexington*, 386 S.W. 2d 738 (Ky. 1964); Louisiana: *Board of Commissioners of Port of New Orleans v. Splendour Shipping and Enterprises*, 273 So. 2d 19 (la. 1973); Maine: *Davies v. City of Bath*, Decision No. 1385. Maine Supreme Court October 12, 1976 A. 2d (1976); Michigan: *Williams v. City of Detroit* 364 Mich. 231, III N.W. 2d 1 (1961); Minnesota: *Spanel v. Mounde View School District No.* 621 264 Minn. 279, 118 N.W. d 795 1962 an *Neiting v. Blondell*, 235 N.W. 2d 597, 599 (Minn. 1975); Nebraska: *Johnson v. Municipal University of Omaha*, 184 Neb. 512, 196 N.W. 2d (1969) and *Brown v. City of Omaha*, 183 Neb. 430, 160 N.W. 2d 805 (1968); Nevada: *Rice v. Clark County*, 79 Nev. 253, 382 P. 2d 605 (1963); New Hampshire: *Merrill v. Manchester*, 114 N.M. 722, 332 A. 2d 378, 382–83 (N.H. 1975); New

In addition to the cases cited by the National Association of Attorneys General, several other state courts have taken action.[14, 15] Some state courts, however, believe that action to limit sovereign immunity should originate in the state legislatures rather than in the courts.

In *Morash and Sone, Inc. v. Commonwealth*, 296 N.E. 2d 461 (Mass. 1973), Davis noted the "unanimity of the Massachusetts court" in deciding this case. In making its decision, the court stated:

> There are pervasive reasons why the governmental immunity doctrine applicable to the Commonwealth and its subdivisions should be abolished. But rather than this court abrogate such doctrine by judicial action, the court recommended "the changes should be accomplished by legislation. The court added: we believe the legislature should be afforded an opportunity to do them by a comprehensive statute." 296 N.E. 2d at 468.[16]

Jersey: *Willes v. Department of Conservation and Economic Development,* 55 N.J. 534, 264 A 2d 34 (1970); New Mexico: *Hicks v. New Mexico* 544. P. 2d 1153, 1155 (N.M. 1975); North Dakota: *Kitto v. Minot Park District,* 224 N.W. 2d (N.D. 1974); Pennsylvania: *Apala v. Philadelphia Board of Public Education,* 305 A. Pa. 973 ; Rhode Island: *Becker v. Beaudoin,* 106. R.I. 562, 761 A. 2d 896 (1970); Tennessee: *Johnson v. Omau Const. Co.,* 519 S.W. 2d 782, 786 (Tenn. 1975); *West Virginia: Long v. Weirton,* 214 S.O. 2d 832, 858 (W. Va.1975); Wisconsin: *Holytz v. City of Milwaukee,* 17 Wis. 2d 26, 115 N.W. 2d 618 (1962). Sovereign Immunity: Liability of Government and its Officials (Raleigh, N.C.: The National Association of Attorneys General, November,1976), pp. 31–33.

14. *Hicks v. State,* 88 N.M. 588, 544 P. 2d 1153 (1976); West Virginia: *Long v. City of Weirton,* 214 S.E. 2d 832 (W.Va. 1975). See Davis, 1 78 Supplement to Administrative Law Practice (San Diego; California: K.C. Davis Publishing Company, 1978), p. 207.

15. Arkansas: *Sturdivant v. City of Farmington,* 255 Ark. 415, 500 S.W.2d 769 (1973); Connecticut: *Lapierre v. Town of Bristol,* 31 Conn.· Supp. 442, 333 A. 2d 710 (1974); Delaware: *Variety Builders, Inc. v. Polikoff,* 305 A. 2d 613 (Del. 1973); Vermont: *Town of Milton v. Brault,* 320 A. 2d 630 (Vt. 1974); Wyoming: *Collins v. Memorial Hospital of Sheridan County,* 521 P. Zd 1339 Wyo. Kenneth Cup Davis, Administrative Law of the Seventies (Rochester, New York: The Lawyers Co Operative Publishing Company, 1976) 551.

16. Davis, 552–553.

In a confronting position to the Massachusetts the Pennsylvania Supreme Court in *Ayala v. Philadelphia Board of Public Education* held "the doctrine of governmental immunity—long since devoid of any valid justification—is abolished in this Commonwealth."[17] The Pennsylvania Court continued:

> We join the ever-increasing number of jurisdictions which have judicially abandoned this antiquated doctrine. The doctrine of governmental immunity—judicially imposed—may be judicially terminated . . . . The cases are numerous in which this court has requested principles which were "out of accord with modern conditions of life." . . . The controlling principle which emerges from these and other decisions is clear—the doctrine of state decisions is not a vehicle for perpetuating error, but rather a legal concept which responds to the demands of justice and thus, permits the unduly growth processes of the law to flourish. 453 Pa. 585, 305 A. Zd 877, 878, 888 (1973).

In a concurring opinion to *Ayala* one justice added:

> The doctrine of governmental immunity is unconstitutional as is the doctrine of sovereign immunity. No branch of government—the executive, the legislative, or the judicial branch—can deprive a citizen of proper redress for a wrong. 453 Pa. 585, 305 A. Zd at 889.

In a decision to abrogate sovereign immunity in Maine, the Supreme Court decided it had given the legislature ample time to abolish the rule. Hence, in *Bath v. City of Davies*, the Maine Supreme Court "laid the doctrine to rest . . . "[18]

---

17. Ibid., 553.

18. Committee on the Office of the Attorneys General. This report notes The Maine Supreme Court . . . had urged the end of sovereign immunity in 1961, said the doctrine was not logical in 1972, and finally announced in 1973 that the legislature should have a reasonable . . . time before we consider whether . . . we should assume the responsibility of abrogating this rule. When three years passed with no legislative action, the court cited numerous court decisions abolishing sovereign immunity . . ..(p. 33).

In explaining the recent spurt of increased activity in the area of immunity abrogation, Davis states "the older law (common law doctrine of sovereign immunity) usually had arrived (activities performed by government but which can also be done by private enterprise[19]). . . .What is meant by abolition is a creation of liability against the government and officials) for torts resulting from governmental functions."[20]

It may be seen, therefore, that the abrogation of immunity could have significant adverse effects on the ability of the government and the public official to continue in the performance of essential functions and duties. In order to avert the harmful effects created by abrogating sovereign immunity state legislatures have responded to judicial abrogation of immunity by either reinstating sovereign immunity in some form or through the adoption of legislation designed to protect the governments, interests and the individual governmental officials. The Committee on the Office of Attorneys General Report cites, for example, "when an Arkansas court abrogated the doctrine of sovereign immunity, the legislature immediately reinstated the doctrine, finding the vitality of the principle essential to the final integrity of the state[21] Davis notes the Arkansas legislature feared bankruptcy.[22] Most states have responded to court decisions, however, by instituting measures to limit the claims and suits filed against the government and governmental officials. Chief of these measures are the Tort Claims Acts. "These acts have the effect of reinstating immunity except where the act provides for liability, although most have fairly broad liability". . . .They commonly include a requirement that all claims be presented to the relevant state department or agency,[23] which is

19. Proprietary functions as defined by the National League of Cities in *The New World of Municipal Liability*, 1.

20. Davis, *Administrative Law of the Seventies*, 553.

21. Committee of the Office of Attorneys General, Statutes Ann., 35 and see Arkansas Sections 12-2901 (Supp. 1969).

22. Davis, *Administrative Law of the Seventies*, 556.

23. Committee on the Office of Attorneys General, *Report*, page 35 and Table 2, "State Liability Legislation," 36–41.

given a specified period of time in which to review the claim and either pay it or deny it. In some states the claimant may seek redress in the court as soon as the claim is denied by the department, as in the Utah Code Ann., Sections 63-30-12. In Iowa, a special hearing or appeal board must review and affirm the denial of the claim before the jurisdiction of a court may be invoked.[24]

It is reported that every tort claims act instituted by a state includes some provisions for exceptions *to* liability. For example, the California Tort Claims Act provides immunity *to* governmental officials for discretionary acts within the scope of employment.[25]

Under the California Act, "a citizen with a claim arising out of governmental activities would, under legal principles, have a cause of action against both the employed who was the proximate cause of the injury or damage," and against the governmental entity employing him under the doctrine of *respondent superior*.[26] As the common law developed *respondent superior* did not apply in the case of a governmental employer. The California Act, however, includes this doctrine and now, "the Act provides that in the absence of fraud, malice, or corruption, the state will represent and indemnify a state employee against whom a claim is brought."[27]

Prior to 1970, abolition of sovereign immunity of state and local governments came primarily from the courts. But since 1970, abolition of the doctrine has come much more from legislatures than from the courts.[28]

---

24. Committee on the Office of Attorneys General, 35.

25. Ibid.

26. As defined by Black, this maxim means that "a master is liable in certain cases for the wrongful acts of his servant. . . . This doctrine is inapplicable where the jury scope of authority." *Respondent Superior* does not apply in relation between state officers and their subordinates, unless superior participates in or directs act. Municipalities are exempt from doctrine when officers are acting in exercise of governmental functions. Henry Campbell Black, *Black's Law Dictionary,* Fourth Edition, Revised. (St. Paul, Minn.: West Publishing 1968).

27. Committee on the Office of Attorneys General, 35.

28. Davis, *Administrative Law of the Seventies,* 554.

As· have been pointed out, generally courts have cited reasons based on jurisdictional grounds that the legislature should have the responsibility for reevaluating sovereign immunity and abrogating it if the legislature saw doing so to be in the best interest of the state. Courts have stated further that the legislature should have time to make changes in the law.[29] Many states have reacted to the complex problem of protecting governments and its officials on the one hand and providing a form of redress to persons injured on the other by governmental actions in at least two ways: they have either abrogated sovereign immunity and limited its coverage or legislatures have responded to the cause with tort claims acts and other forms of legislation designed to reduce the threat of personal liability and provide a channel through which injured plaintiffs could receive compensation for their damages.

In the development of tort claims acts, the National League of Cities reports,[30] most legislature "attempts involve placing dollar limits on claims and granting except in cases of malfeasance or As of 1978, thirty-six of the states that had adopted or were considering tort reform legislation had established, or prepared to establish, dollar limits on claims.[31]

The National League of Cities has analyzed the features of the Oklahoma Tort Claims Act of 1978. According to its report, one feature of the Oklahoma law is that it attempts to cope with individual federal civil liability as much as possible through state legislation. The report further states that the Oklahoma laws "require the city government to be responsible for defending employees or officers who are sued under federal law" and to pay any judgment that might be awarded "so long as the employee or officer acted in good faith."[32] Other legislative initiatives in several states have included provisions for liability insurance and variously related arrangements. In 1977, Oregon and Colorado, for example, adopted initiatives authorizing broad "powers for municipalities

29. Ibid.
30. National League of Cities, 6.
31. Ibid.
32. Ibid., 7.

to insure, self-insure, establish reserves, and cooperate with other governments for meeting insurance needs."[33]

Although the Commonwealth of Virginia adheres to the traditional common law doctrine of sovereign immunity, it has taken legislative action to alleviate some of the undesirable effects of personal liability suits.[34] In the 1976 session of the General Assembly, legislators adopted legislation providing that

> Any school board may provide liability insurance, or may provide self-insurance, for certain or all of its officers and employees and for student teachers and other persons performing functions or services for any school in the division, even though such persons performing functions or services without payment· therefor, to cover negligent acts committed or alleged to have been committed while discharging their duties or performing functions or services for a school.[35] (Code of Virginia Ann., Section 22–56.2)

Also, in the 1978 Session of the General Assembly, the legislature passed House Joint Resolution No. 176 which established a Joint Subcommittee to study the insurance problem of localities within the State. The Resolution authorized the subcommittee to "examine all serious insurance problems of localities" with particular attention to liability insurance for public officials.[36]

In prior sessions, the Virginia legislature passed statutes which to some degree have held the number of liability suits against public officials to a minimum and, consequently, have minimized the effects of personal liability lawsuits. Of all the statutes passed, Section 15.1–506.1 is possibly the most important to local public

33. Ibid.

34. For example, see "Torts," 59 *Virginia Law Review* 1617–1619 (May 1973).

35. Dobbins, 11.

36. Commonwealth of Virginia, *Initial Staff Study for Joint Subcommittee Study in Insurance Problems of Localities*, Virginia Division of Legislative Services, 1978.

officials. It provides for liability insurance for officers and employees of Virginia counties, cities and towns.[37]

Just how much the State is concerned about personal liability of public officials in Virginia's local governments is indicated by the Virginia legislature's adoption in 1974 of two House Joint Resolutions, Numbers 20 and 124. Both Resolutions authorized the Committee for Courts of Justice to study the doctrine of sovereign immunity and determine methods for reducing the impact of personal liability suits against public officials.[38]

Before adopting HJR 20, the Virginia legislature considered several reasons why it should study or reexamine the doctrine of governmental immunity which has become "firmly imbedded in the common law of the Commonwealth."[39] It cited the fact that "the majority of states have abolished the doctrine, either judicially or legislatively, as being outmoded and unfair."[40] The legislature noted that "while the Supreme Court of Virginia has consistently upheld the doctrine, in some of the opinions it has strongly hinted that the General Assembly should exercise its prerogatives, and take a sharp, close look at the problem."[41] As worded in the Resolution, the 1974 General Assembly recognized that the doctrine of sovereign immunity "often results in uncompensated loss to individuals who can ill afford such loss and through no fault of their own." The legislature also was aware that the United States had a federal tort claims act and, therefore, decided to study the problem

---

37. Specifically, this Section provides: The board of supervisors or school board of any county and the governing body of any political or governmental subdivision may provide liability insurance, or may provide self-insurance, for certain or all of its officers and employees to cover the costs and expenses incident *to* liability, including those for settlement, suit or satisfaction of judgment, arising from the conduct of its officials and employees in the discharge of their duties. Code of Virginia, Section 15.1–506.1.

38. Commonwealth of Virginia, *Report of the Senate and House Committees for Courts of Justice on Governmental Immunity to the Governor and the General Assembly of Virginia-House Document Number 31*, (1975).

39. Ibid.

40. Ibid.

41. Ibid.

of governmental immunity "with a view to adoption of a State tort claim act" on the order of the Federal model.

The Subcommittee completed its study by Fall 1974. The 1975 General Assembly, however, did not act on the study; several questions remained unanswered. The Subcommittee found, first, that there was no acceptable method or alternative by which the doctrine of sovereign immunity and governmental immunity could be replaced. Second, lacking a specific legislative proposal, the Subcommittee was unable to provide sufficient data pertaining to the cost of tort claims legislation in Virginia. The Subcommittee's most visible achievement was a "draft" Tort Claims Act For Virginia.[42]

As early as 1941, George Warp recognized the difficulty in producing legislation which would reduce the thrust of liability suits against public officials and also compensate persons injured by the government or a public official.[43] According to Warp, some writers have advocated legislation designed to reduce or abolish the customary immunity of municipalities. But Warp notes "the task of drafting such legislation is not easy . . . Laws must be dreamt up which will not only meet the situation fairly for the litigant, but which will also protect the public purse from spurious claims and skyrocketed damages."[44] Warp draws from another scholar who helps to explain why some states, like Virginia, have been slow in adopting tort claims legislation.[45]

> The greatest difficulty arises out of the limited resources of the small town or city. Their representatives in the legislature will oppose the enlargement of communal liability, for a single accident might ruin them. But in as much as experience indicates that most injuries occur in connection with traffic or highways, much of which is

42. See Commonwealth of Virginia, *House Document No. 31.*

43. Warp, "Municipal Tort Liability in Virginia," *Report of the Bureau of Public Administration*, Page 61.

44. Ibid.

45. Warp, *Recent Statutory Developments in Municipal Liability in Tort* (1936 2 Leg. Notes on Loc.Govt. 9 too.

not local at all, that the state might appropriately take over the major part of the tort liability of small communities and limit the local liability for a given percentage of the local revenues.

In order to protect the local government from damaging liability suits, Warp suggests

> Probably the liability should at the beginning be limited in property cases to $25,000 and.in personal injury or death to $7,500 or $10,000. Injuries should not be permitted, a short statute of limitation should be provided, and attorney's fees should be limited. The greatest difficulty arises in suggesting a system of procedural administration, so as to afford simple yet effective means of redress, while fully safe-guarding the defenses of the community.

Several states have adopted tort claims legislation and several writers and scholars have generally supported this type of legislation. While Virginia has yet to adopt a State Tort Claims Act, it seems likely that, once the unresolved issues surrounding the abrogation of sovereign immunity are settled, this legislation will be available to Virginia localities and public officials.

The Liability Insurance Alternative

Since the Virginia General Assembly has not been able to draft any tort claims legislation which is acceptable for adoption, many localities within the Commonwealth have tried to insure themselves and their public officials against the adverse effects of liability lawsuits. Liability insurance for many localities, however, has not proven to be a lasting and feasible alternative. In writing about the insurance problem, the National League of Cities notes:

> Cities have not been viewed as good liability risks by commercial risk bearers—insurance companies. They advance a number of reasons for this point of view. Disappearing immunity and an ill-defined scope of tort laws increase exposure and create unpredictable

risks. . . . Legal limitations on the amount of liability insurance that can be written by a carrier is another reason
sometimes cited as a contributor to the commercial carriers' inability to write policies. Higher claims, supposed-
ly out of portion premiums, may also be an influence.[46]

While several other reasons may have some bearing on the
problem, it appears to the NLC that "resource shrinkage and
unpredictable markets are probably the real causes of the insurance problem."[47] Apparently, as a result of the 1973–74 recession,
reserves of many insurance firms have shrunk, and therefore,
companies are not[48] able to write as many policies as they did before. Some insurance companies may be able but are not willing to
insure local governments and their public officials against liability
suits at the same insurance rates as they did a year or so ago. William Peet, an Insurance Consultant for the League of Minnesota
Cities believes that the insurance industry has created a false im-
pression in the marketplace so as to raise premiums. He notes:

> There are indications from more than one source to
> raise a suspicion that the increase in the cost of liability
> insurance this past year (1976) or so has not been due
> to any increase in successful claims against insurers for
> malpractice or products, but may have been brought
> about by manipulation of insurers of scare headlines in
> the press.[49]

Two other writers note that several problems have created rising premium insurance.[50] For whatever the reasons it is

46. National League of Cities, 4.

47. Ibid., 4–6.

48. Ibid., 4.

49. *A Nationwide Problem: Putting Perspective. The Risks of Liability for Public Officials and for Everybody Else.* William Peet, League of Minnesota Cities, page 1.

50. Howard G. Camden and Richard L. Heskin, both of the Advanced Underwriters Insurance Agency, Inc., cite eight reasons for rising insurance premiums: double digit inflation; a claims-conscious public; the dramatically rising cost of medical care; the public's attitude towards municipalities; the erosion of governmental immunity; aggressiveness of plaintiffs' attorneys; the

unfortunate for local governments that this phenomenon number of liability suits filed against public officials is increasing[51] and many budgets are shrinking as a result of inflation and taxpayer resistance to an increasing tax burden. While most localities liability insurance, automobile liability and law enforcement liability insurance for several years, many have only recently begun to carry liability insurance for their public officials and other governmental employees. Some localities have never purchased official liability insurance either because the premiums were too high or a willing insurer has been difficult to find. Of these localities which have been successful in obtaining official liability insurance, some have seen their policies pulled for seemingly nothing.[52] The problem of obtaining personal liability insurance is compounded by the fact that many states are abrogating immunity at a time when there is a "growing willingness to sue."[53, 54] As a result of decisions and acts by the courts and state legislatures, there are now fewer barriers to filing suits against public officials and government. The NLC report states:

---

tendency of courts to give verdicts far in excess of injuries sustained; and municipal insurance has been underpriced for year . See Camden and Heskin, "A Look at the Crisis In Municipal Insurance," *Michigan Municipal Review*, (July 1977), p. 126.

51. See Nester Roos, "Public Official Liability: 1976," *Urban Data Service Reports,* Vol. 9, No. 5 (Washington, DC: International City Management Association, May 1977), 1–6 and "Liability of Council Members for Violation of Civil Rights," *Illinois Municipal Review,* (February 1976), 4.

52. This is more alarming since, in at least one local government (Arlington County), no claims or suits were reported. Letter from Thomas Parker, Arlington County Insurance Administrator to Hugh (Chip)Fisher, Legislature Research Associate, Virginia Division of Legislative Services, dated May 9, 1978.

53. National League of Cities, 3.

54. The state of affairs is summarized in an article in *Western City*: The increase in suits against government entities is a reflection of the liability explosion and the litigation boom in general. "If someone is hurt, somebody has to pay for it" seems to be the order of the day. "The Municipal Liability Insurance Crises—An Overview," *Western City,* (October 1976), 36.

> Suing is a means to right an individual or social wrong and is often accompanied by the "limitless pocketbook" notion. Large institutions, such as cities are perceived as having lots of money.[55]

As a result of inflationary insurance premiums and the unwillingness of insurance firms to accept calculated degrees of risk, local governments still face the problem of how to protect their public officials from being personally liable to a claimant. There are several alternative measures being studied which may help to relieve the threat of personal liability and also be less burdensome on the fiscal capacity of the community.[56]

There are basically three types of insurance coverage or some form of liability control measures now being made available to local governments. They are the "pool concept," "risk management," and "self-insurance." As proposed in California (1975), the "pool concept" is a type of insurance coverage which is designed to include several or all of local governments in an insurance pool.[57] The purpose of the arrangement is to "spread risks, paying into the pool on much the same basis as premiums are purchased from commercial carriers."[58]

This alternative was dropped in California since the insurance scheme required the participation of insurance firms operating within that state; "there was little or no interest on the part of the carriers to establish a pool . . ."[59] New approaches, such as "pooled insurance arrangements among groups of local governments or in

---

55. National League of Cities, 4.

56. Bradley K. Harmes notes:"there are several non-traditional options available, (including) 'self insurance', 'high deductible', 'pooling', 'reciprocal arrangement' and 'captive insurance.'"Memorandum to Richard L. DeCair, Executive Director, Virginia Municipal League, from Harmes, Senior Staff Associate - VML, RE: Insurance Seminar, dated June 9, 1978.

57. The Municipal Liability Insurance Crisis—An Overview", *Western City* (October 1976), p. 6.

58. NLC, 13.

59. "The Municipal Insurance Crisis--An Overview," 6.

cooperation with the State," are being considered in several states including Virginia.[60]

"Risk Management" is not a type of insurance; rather, it is an administrative task designed to identify causes of liability and determine the most effective and least costly means of alleviating losses as may arise from claims filed against local governments or their officials. Risk Management is defined in one article as "a conscious attempt to minimize the adverse effects of risks, at minimum cost, through its identification, measurement and control."[61] Rising private insurance premiums have spurred several states to adopt legislation which provides for another alternative, self-insurance programs.[62] As reported, "with self-insurance, a city insures itself or insures against risk through maintenance of financial reserves for repaying losses."[63] A governmental decision to leave "small recurrent losses uninsured is a form of self-insurance."[64] Before adopting a self-insurance program; a city for example, must determine what types of losses to self insure. It must consider and determine the impact a loss or several recurring losses could have on fiscal capacity. The effectiveness of self-insurance as a hedge

---

60. Advisory Commission on Intergovernmental Relations,"States Tackle Tough Fiscal Issues," *Intergovernmental Perspective*, Vol. 5, No. 1 (Winter 1979), p.22.

61. "A Guide to the Management of Liability Risk for the Public Institution," Florida Association of Insurance Agents, (October 1974) cited in "Liability Insurance for Florida Cities," *Florida Municipal Record*, (January 1977), 7.

62. According to the Advisory Commission on Intergovernmental Relations (ACIR), "In 1978, at least six states adopted legislation allowing local governments to self-insure or develop inter-local insurance pools:" Missouri, Iowa, Ohio, Oklahoma, Virginia and Wisconsin. *Intergovernmental Perspective*, Vol. 5, No. 1 (Winter 1979), p. 22. See also The National Association of Attorneys General Report, p 82.

63. NLC, 13.

64. Richard Aronson and Eli Schwartz, *Management Policies in Local Government Finance* (Washington, DC: International City Management Association, 1975), p. 276.

against official liability fund the city can build up to pay off its losses."[65]

One writer warns:

> Self-insurance is a tremendous gamble; the small community should undertake such a self-insurance program only in extremely low-risk areas. That is, the community should only self-insure those activities where the judgments if incurred would not be extravagant, and those activities which have a very low probability of municipal liability.[66]

There are several advantages and disadvantages or limitations to each alternative. Of course, risk management is not an insurance alternative. It provides a type of "preventative maintenance" and "costs money."[67] A risk manager may be employed specifically for this task or the task may be given to the Director of Finance. In some cases, a contract with a private insurance agent may be desirable. In any case, the manager must have a thorough knowledge of the operation and facilities of the locality and be able to communicate effectively with all officials. An effective program must also have funds available for personnel training, i.e., workshops and seminars.[68]

According to the National League of Cities report, "self-insuring on an individual city basis or through cooperation pools is not a simple solution. Cities and states creating these instruments are facing, or will face the same problems that plague the commercial carriers—indeterminate legislation, poor data, and difficult or impossible loss predictions."[69] More important, however, is the question of whether self-insurance will protect the public official from the chilling effects of personal liability suits. With the self-insurance program having to be funded each year as any other

---

65. Gary Christian, "Minimize Losses and Cut Premiums," *Alabama Municipal Journal*, (December 1975), p. 24.

66. Ibid.

67. NLC, 13.

68. See Christian, 6–7,24.

69. NLC, 13.

expenditure . . . on the basis of political and economic consider-
ations, it is questionable as to whether the funds will be available
at the time needed.[70]

Liability insurance may be less desirable under any alternative knowing that the presence of the coverage may prompt a court
to declare a local government amenable to suit.[71] In other words,
a court may waive immunity, even in the absence of an approved
tort claims act or established limits on liability. Another problem
associated with insurance protection is "the knowledge that there
is an insurance coverage with monies available for damages may
actually increase the frequency of suits against public officials."[72]

Although there are several disadvantages to the liability insurance alternative, there are at present no other arrangements
which protect the public official with this degree of assurance that
funds will be available to pay off claims at the time needed. In
Virginia's search for alternatives, the Virginia Municipal League is
looking at alternatives which include reciprocal, self-funded pool
and other group insurance concepts. Until these arrangements are

70. George R. St. John, Albemarle County attorney, has reservations that
"self-insurance" is a desirable strategy for providing personal liability coverage
for public officials. In a letter to William A. Broaddus, Esq., County Attorney
for Henrico County, St. John notes: My thinking is that if this (self-insurance
program) appropriation is not spent in a given fiscal year, it must be re-appro-
priated each year, and no board of supervisors is bound by its predecessors to
make an appropriation. You are therefore no more certain of having on hand
appropriated monies to pay a judgment against a county official after the first
year in which the program is established, than you would be if you simply
waited until after a judgment is entered, and then ask the board to make the
necessary appropriations. Letter to William A. Broaddus, Esq. from George R.
St. John, Attorneys At Law, Charlottesville, Virginia, dated June 23, 1977. Re:
Self-insurance Program-File# ACG 77-352.

71. William Broaddus and Frederick v. Payne, Deputy County Attorney-
Albemarle, are among several Virginia lawyers and political scientists who
have analyzed liability insurance, and whose findings are supportive of this
statement. See, for example, a copy of a Memorandum from Payne to George
R. St. John, RE. "Liability Insurance Self-Insurance," dated June 15, 1977.
George R. St. John Associates, Attorneys At Law, Charlottesville, Virginia (Insurance Files).

72. Kenneth Henning, "Liability of City Officials," *Texas Town and City*
(October 1975), p. 8.

accepted and approved by the League and the member local governments, public officials must continue to rely on the individual local government's insurance mode.

The Indemnification Concept and Its Limitations

The third alternative, indemnification, is similar to, and may be considered a type of liability insurance for the public official. Whereas, under most liability insurance policies, "The insurer, almost invariably a company engaged in the business, undertakes to indemnify the insured against a loss which he may sustain through payments made by reason of his becoming legally liable to a third person, . . . " the indemnification concept means that a defendant official of the government, sued by reason of his employment, is reimbursed for all costs paid out of pocket.[73]

Some states have statutes whereby an official may be indemnified.[74] In 1978, the Virginia General Assembly amended Section 15.1–19.2 of the Code of Virginia which provides: "all costs and expenses of (legal) proceeding (which names as defendants, any member, officer, employee, trustee or board or commission member) . . . by virtue of any actions in furtherance of their duties in serving such county, city, town or political subdivision shall be charged against the treasury of the county, city, town or political subdivision and shall be paid out of funds provided therefor by the governing body thereof." Indemnification is limited to public officials sued in their official capacity or sued because of acts committed within the official scope of responsibility.[75] As the courts have applied the concept, generally no person may be indemnified where the acts of the official are not in the discharge of his duties to the governing body or if the act accused of was done maliciously within the scope of his duties.[76] Indemnification may be limited also depending on the court's view of the case and the legislative

---

73. Prosser, *The Law of Torts*, 541–42.

74. See National Association of Attorneys General, 91–98.

75. Ibid., 92G.

76 See Rhyne, et al., 324.

provisions.[77] The indemnification concept is designed to achieve the social object to an individual injured by the act(s) of the public official while, at the same time, removing much of the threat of personal liability or financial loss from the conscience of the public official. For the most part, this objective is difficult to satisfy. In order for a plaintiff to secure a judgment against the official, he must "allege and prove that the action that the official took was a malicious one or one that was outside the scope of the official's authority."[78] Such a determination and finding by the court will usually "mean that the municipality under its indemnification statute or ordinance does not have to indemnify that official."[79] The plaintiff is thus left with his damage judgment against the defendant public official[80] who is then personally liable for damages as may be awarded by the court. Several states have developed various measures to alleviate the harmful aspects of personal liability suits against public officials.

Many of these measures have been developed in the wake or in reaction to the in creasing number of suits against the government and governmental officials. These acts, mostly legislative and judicial, are "identified as some of the potential effects of personal liability suits against the public official. Three measures or alternatives designed to alleviate the threat of personal liability have been analyzed in this chapter.

One or all three are either being considered or used in several states, including Virginia. Of the three measures or concepts, an act to limit or abrogate sovereign immunity with the establishment of a tort claims act appears to be the most desirable. Within the limits of the tort claims legislation, an injured plaintiff could bring a suit against the public official or the government since neither the official nor the government would be immune from suit. An acceptable tort claims act would technically provide official immunity for discretionary acts within the scope of employment.

77. National Association of Attorneys General, 93.
78. Rhyne, et al., 335.
79. Ibid.
80. Ibid.

By defining the acts by which a suit may be brought against the official, tort claims legislation would eliminate the need for personal liability insurance. Liability insurance for the government, however, could be made available for suits against it.

In the absence of tort claims legislation, liability insurance for public officials and indemnification concepts are acceptable alternatives. These alternatives provide some measure of protection for the public official from the adverse effects of liability suits and are available to local governments and public officials in Virginia.

The Effects of a Liability Suit:
Fleming v. Albemarle County Board of Supervisors[81]

Several scholars and writers on the subject of governmental and official liability have identified various forms of effects as a result of liability suits against the government and the governmental official. One writer[82] notes that there has been "a dramatic rise in the dollar amount of damages awarded or settled in such suits."[83] This writer also notes "accountability for decisions is broadening substantially" and "more stringent requirements for claiming im-

81. 577 F. 2d 236 (1978).

82. Kenneth Henning reports: Recently (1975) the news media reported an award of $12 million damages against the District of Columbia government and the chiefs of the metropolitan and capital police force in actions arising out of the 1971 "preventive detention" arrests of anti-war demonstrators in the nation's capital; an out-of court settlement of $750,000 by a city government and a former police officer in connection with an action charging false arrest and imprisonment; court confirmation of a damage award of $85,000 against several county officials for negligently failing to issue regulations for the operation of a prison farm in a case where a juvenile prisoner was permanently blinded when a trustee guard shot him with a shotgun; an award of $40,000 against a police officer who had shot a juvenile in the course of a civil disorder; a United States Supreme Court affirmation of a Federal District Court award of $7,200 damages against an official of a state government who had disapproved the hiring of a racially-mixed couple; and a Federal District Court award of $6,000 damages against three former city aldermen for violating the civil rights of a property owner by denying his zoning request.

83. Henning, 4.

munity are being imposed."[84] Of course, as previously noted, official liability suits usually encourage individuals and institutions affected by them to find a means to avoid them.

When a public official liability suit is filed against a board of supervisors, city, or town council, or against the governing body and the individual member, the impact of the suit is felt to some extent by the entire community; it has both financial and political implications. Depending on how the case is viewed a suit may paralyze the government since any action the governing body takes may be a conflict of interest. The case presented here is an example of a tremendously involved suit, involving the Albemarle County Board of Supervisors, the board members in their individual and official capacity, two interest groups (Citizens of Albemarle, Inc., and Albemarle County Taxpayers, Inc.), several concerned individuals, and James N. Fleming, et al. who became the principal plaintiff or appellee in the lawsuit(s). The facts and opinions for this case are derived from the briefs and petitions presented by the lawyers for the various parties, orders and decisions of the United States (Western) District Court-Virginia and the Court of Appeals for the Fourth Circuit, and *Federal Reporter, 2d Series.* Newspaper accounts of developments in this case and other memoranda also support the findings of this case study.

The Fleming suit(s) against the Albemarle County Board of Supervisors and other parties began *to* form on or about October 1973, when James N. Fleming, Flemenco Enterprises, Inc. and Four Seasons West[85] filed a rezoning application with the Albemarle County Planning Commission. Fleming requested that a tract of land, some 128 acres, located on Hydraulic Road, approximately onehalf mile from the intersection of Hydraulic Road and Rio Road, near the South (Fork) Rivanna River in Albemarle

84. According to Henning, "public decisions rendered in private by small groups of entrenched elected officials, political appointees, and self-appointed 'leaders,' which violate rights, privileges, and immunities guaranteed by the United States Constitution and statutory law, are increasingly being challenged and remedied as a consequence of new federal laws, national mobility . . . (etc.)." 4.

85. Cited hereinafter as "Fleming."

County, Virginia, be rezoned for a planned unit development (PUD)[86] Fleming sought zoning approval for the development of a "moderate-income, racially-integrated residential community" *to* be known as "Evergreen."[87] The "Evergreen" plan as originally submitted in conjunction with the rezoning application was not acceptable *to* the planning staff or planning commission. After being revised on several occasions and, finally, approved by the planning commission, the matter came before the Board of Supervisors, over a year later, on January 22, 1975.[88] A public hearing was held on the plan and, after "much discussion and opposition *to* Evergreen by various persons and groups both from Albemarle County and the City of Charlottesville,"[89] the Board closed the meeting and continued the matter *to* February 12, 1975.[90] On February 12, the Board of Supervisors "unanimously denied approval of Evergreen."[91]

86. Appendix for Appellants, *Citizens for Albemarle, Inc. and Albemarle Count Tax payers, Inc. v. James, et al.* No. 76-0 Cir. 77.

87. Brief for Appellees, *Citizens for Albemarle, et al. v. Fleming,* No. 76-2308 (4th Cir. 1977).

88. As noted in the Complaint of the original suit, "when the matter came before the defendant Board of Supervisors, plaintiffs informed defendants that it would be willing *to* abide with all the conditions established by the staff *except* the condition of a 2.5 dwelling units per acre density, explaining that a 2.5 density requirement would drive the cost of each unit out of economic reach of and would make construction and sales so prohibitively expensive as *to* exclude virtually all lower and middle income group persons" (Emphasis in original). See Appendix for Appellants, *Citizens for Albemarle.*

89. In a discussion on the opposition of the planned development focused primarily on the project's environ mental impact on the Rivanna Reservoir, the main source of public water supply for parts of Albemarle County and the City of Charlottesville. See Appendix for Appellants, Citizens for Albemarle.

90. Appendix for Appellants; *Citizens for Albermarle.*

91. Ibid.

On March 17, 1975,[92] Fleming filed suit in the Federal court[93] against Albemarle County, the Board of Supervisors, and each member of the Board, individually, and in his official capacity.[94] Fleming brought action against the County and Board members for "declaratory, and injunctive relief as well as monetary damage to redress the injury done to (him) by defendants' policies and practices of discriminating against plaintiff under color of state law based on race and color of plaintiffs by arbitrarily and capriciously denying plaintiffs' request . . .[95] For the several violations of his rights, Fleming demanded judgment against the defendants, each of them jointly and severally in the amount of $1,000,000 and that the Court award, in addition, "costs and attorneys' fees against -the defendants and grant such other relief as is necessary, proper, and equitable for the resolution of this cause."[96]

In a subsequent action, Albemarle County, the Board of Supervisors, and the members, individually, and in their official capacities filed a "Motion To Dismiss"[97] *Fleming* " . . . because the

92. As of March 17, there was a suit pending in a court of the Commonwealth of Virginia involving Fleming and the Albemarle board of Supervisors. On March 7,1975, Fleming filed suit in the Albemarle Circuit Court against the Board of Supervisors petitioning the Court (the Honorable Judge David Berry, Judge of the Court, presiding) to declare the Board abused its power in denying the rezoning application and that the Board's action was "illegal, discriminatory, arbitrary, capricious, unlawful, without substantial relation to public health, safety and general welfare, and should be reversed." In essence, Fleming asked the Court to request the Board of Supervisors to reconsider its action.

93. Clerk's Office, In the United States District Court for the Western District of Virginia Charlottesville Division. The case invoked the jurisdiction of this Court pursuant to the Fourteenth Amendment of the United States Constitution and the United States Code Annotated (U.S.C.), Titles 29 and 42, including Section 1983.

94. Board members named in this suit were Lloyd F. Wood, Stuart F. Carwile, Gordon L. Wheeler, Gerald E. Fisher, William C. Thacker, Jr., and J. T. Henley, Jr.

95. Appendix for Appellants, *Citizens for Albermarle*.

96. Ibid.

97. The "Motion to Dismiss" the suit against the Board and members was filed by George R. St. John, Albemarle County Attorney, Counsel for

Court lacks jurisdiction over the persons of the Defendants in that they are as a matter of law immune from the liability asserted against them by the plaintiffs" and because" . . . the subject matter in and the facts underlying the complaint are substantially identical to those which form the basis of a suit by the same plaintiffs, asking for substantially the same relief, which is now pending in the Circuit Court of Albemarle County, Virginia."[98]

In answer to the Board of Supervisors' request for the suit to be dismissed, Fleming filed a "Memorandum of Law In Opposition to Defendants' Motion to Dismiss . . ." stating, "the court does not lack jurisdiction over the persons of the defendants because they are not immuned[99] from liability . . . The counsel for Fleming cites in support of its argument *Jones v. Diamond*, 519 F. 2d 1090 (1975) and *Schiff v. Williams*, 519 F. 2d 257 (1975) for the authority that "public officials may be sued under the 42 U.S.C. 1983 for monetary damages, as well as equitable relief under certain circumstances, despite the concept of immunity, sovereign or executive."[100] Of course, counsel for the Board filed an "Answer" claiming "the Court is without jurisdiction to grant money damages as to the members of the Board of Supervisors in that they are, as a matter of law, immune."[101]

The arguments for and against *Fleming* were brought to a head on April 26, 1976, when the United States District Court, Chief Judge James C. Turk presiding, ordered the Fleming case dismissed with approval of the planned unit development. Approval

---

Defendants, In the U.S. District Court, Charlottesville, April 7, 1975. The "Motion to Dismiss" cited seven reasons why the Fleming suit should be dismissed. Five of the reasons have less bearing on this research than the two noted in the text and therefore, are not noted here.

98. See Case No. 75–11.

99. Ibid. See also the discussion on "Personal Liability under the Civil Rights Act of 1871 (42 U.S.G. Section 1983)" in the preceding chapter 3.

100. Counsel for the plaintiffs also cites *Scheuer v. Rhodes*, 416 U.S. 232 (1974) in which the Supreme Court held that the executive immunity of the Governor of Ohio against monetary damage claims under Section 1983 was not absolute but qualified.

101. Appendix for Appellants, *Citizens for Albemarle*.

of the development was conditional on plaintiff's development of "Evergreen" at a density of 2.5 units per acre, rather than on 6.7 units per acre as were originally sought. Judge Turk ordered also that the proposed development comply with existing laws and. ordinances currently in effect in Albemarle County.[102]

The foregoing recount of events of *Fleming* are presented to illustrate the progression of the case as it developed over a period of three or more years. As involved as it may appear many of the behind-the-scenes deliberations which influenced the April 26, 1976 decision have been omitted up to this point. Attention must now be focused on some of these deliberations; they are significantly related to the thesis of this research.

On September 19, 1975, following the Albemarle County Planning Commission's approval of the rezoning application, the then (1975) Board of Supervisors and Fleming met and it appeared that the two parties had reached an agreement on "Evergreen. Why the "new" Board rescinded the former Board's action or ignored the existence of a satisfactory agreement between the two parties apparently is a question of politics.[103]

A second deliberation or compromise decision came as a result of a conference which took place in Judge Turk's chambers on April 22, 1976, when the judge accused the new Board of "hanky-panky" and cautioned the individual members of the Board that they had a potential individual (personal) liability in the amount of $1 million for Fleming's alleged damages.[104] Furthermore, Board

102. On April 26, 1976, the Albemarle Board of Supervisors and Fleming signed a consent order in which the Supervisors agreed to approve the plaintiffs' application subject to the condition cited in Turk's order. Ten days later, however, the Citizens for Albemarle, Inc. and Albemarle County Taxpayers, Inc. moved to intervene as parties of the defendant. This action delayed final approval of the proposed development. And as of September 1978, the Fleming application for "Evergreen" had not been approved by the Albemarle County Board. See· *Fleming v. Bedford Moore, et al.*, No. 76-0053(C), (W.D. Va., Filed February 14, 1978).

103. The "new" Board took office January 1, 1976. All but two members, J. T. Henley, Jr. and Gerald E. Fisher, were new members to the Board.

104. *Fleming v. Albemarle County*, No. 75-11-C, (W.D. Va., Filed August 11, 1977); *Fleming v. Citizens for Albemarle, Inc.*, 577 F. 2d 236 (1978)at 38.

members were told they could be personally liable for damages if they refused to approve the amended rezoning application. It is alleged this threat, in particular, coming from the judge, prompted the new Board to approve the proposed development.[105]

Another factor or combination of factors which had some bearing on the April 26 settlement came as a result of the November 1975 general election when three of the five incumbent Board members who sought reelection were defeated at the polls. The unsuccessful encumberits and the one Board member who chose not to seek reelection subsequently were dismissed from the suit; and the new members were made parties to the cause. This change in personalities on the Board, along with their differences in political philosophy or values, may have helped bring the settlement.

As noted in the beginning of this section a suit against the government or against members of the governing body not only affects the governmental unit; it may affect also the entire governmental process, particularly in terms of community's response or reaction to the decisions of the governing body. When a decision is made which, to some extent, benefits a personal interest or a particular group interest to the detriment of others, a potentially explosive situation is created. Parties aggrieved by the decision therefore may file suit(s) against the officials or the government in an effort to satisfy their interests or to express displeasure with actions of the government or public official(s).[106] This problem is

105. Following the Board's consent on April 26 to approve the Fleming application, a suit was filed against Fleming by the Albemarle County Taxpayers and the Citizens for Albemarle, intervenors, in behalf of Albemarle County and the Board of Supervisors. In this suit, the parties defendant (Albemarle County Taxpayers, et al) asserted" . . . that the individual defendants an irreconcilable conflict of interest was created which made it impossible for the individuals, or their defense counsel, to represent the defendants, Albemarle County Virginia and the Board of Supervisors . . .." *Fleming v. Albemarle*, No. 75-ll(C), W.D. Va., Filed August 14, 1976).

106. See *Fleming v. Bedford Moore, et al.*, No. 76-0053 (C), (W.D. Va., Filed February 14, 1978) in which Fleming alleges that "Bedford and Jane Moore formulated a plan of opposition to the special use permit by the County, motivated by racial animus against Fleming and potential black occupants of the Evergreen development." (The Moores own and will reside on property

even more acute when several different individual and group interests are concentrated within a community in a relatively small area. A similar situation is created in largely populated areas where there are usually many different interests and persuasions.

The two organized interest groups which became parties to *Fleming* reacted somewhat differently to the April 26 settlement than the plaintiff, Fleming. Albemarle County Taxpayers and the Citizens for Albemarle strongly claimed that the decision to approve Evergreen was an irresponsible act on the part of the Board of· Supervisors; primarily, because approval of the development was against the interests of the two groups and against many of the residents of Albemarle County whom the groups claimed to represent.[107] This analysis of *Fleming v. Albemarle* was designed to show some of the effects of a personal liability suit against public officials. In the process of developing this analysis, several implications surfaced and have been presented; all of which are related to the thesis.

At least one point of interest may be drawn from this analysis and developed further. That is, while there was a degree of conflict

adjoining the Evergreen site, known as "Shack Mountain.") Judge Turk dismissed the case on grounds that "the evidence presented here does not support an inference of racial animus on the part of the Moores." He furthermore supported his Order to Dismiss on a finding that the Moores "have consistently opposed high density development in the neighboring areas at least since 1965, by white owners as well as by Fleming."

107. On May 6, 1976, ten days after Evergreen was given conditional approval, the two groups filed suit to intervene, praying for a new trial for *Fleming*. On August 10, 1976, the "interventors" suit came to trial in the Federal District Court Charlottesville Division; and the interventors motion for a new trial was denied by Judge Turk, on the grounds that the suit failed to meet the "timeliness requirements" of the Federal Rules of Civil Procedure. Brief for Appellants, *Citizens for Albemarle Inc. and Albemarle Count Tax payers, Inc. v. James N. Fleming, et al.*, No. th Cir.9 . Following Judge Turk's order, Citizens for Albemarle, et al. appealed to the United States Court of Appeals for the Fourth Circuit. The case came to trial and was argued March 9, 1978 and decided June 12, 1978, before Albert V. Bryan, Senior Circuit Judge, Butzer and Widener, Circuit Judges. The Circuit Court reversed the August lOth order by Judge Turk and ordered the District Court to allow the intervention, with additional information or testimony as may be necessary. *Fleming v. Citizens for Albemarle*, 577 F. 2d (1978) at 239.

of interest on the part of the "new" Albemarle Board of Supervisors in making the decision to settle the Evergreen controversy, the board did not cease to function as a governing body on matters relating to the rezoning. In light of the matter involving personal loss (or gain) it is conceivable that the courts could have prohibited the Board members from making any decisions that were related to *Fleming*.[108] However, this does not appear to have been an important consideration to the courts.

A final point of interest found in examining the case, and related to the title of this work, is that while Board members were considered potentially individually liable for damages to Fleming in the amount of $200,000 each, this threat was not sufficient to cause them to not seek reelection. Of the six former Board members—all of whom were named in the original suit—five sought reelection. This would suggest that a potential personal liability suit, in and of itself, has little if any effect on the public official in terms of his overall willingness to serve or continue to serve.

Public Officials' Reactions
to Personal Liability Suits

The effects of personal liability suits against government officials are reduced to some extent by the safeguards of liability insurance, indemnification, and the prospect of a State-enacted Tort Claims Act. The threat of a public official liability suit is reduced further so long as the public official acts within the legislative province. It is within the area of administrative functions that the degree of immunity is qualified or determined by the courts, and therefore, more uncertain.

At the present time, the State of Virginia adheres to the doctrine of sovereign immunity. As long as the doctrine holds,

108. See Va. Code Ann., Section 2.1–352 (Cum. Supp.1976); and Introduction *supra* note 11. James E. Treakle, Jr. Assistant Commonwealth Attorney, Albemarle County, is of the opinion that each individual member of the Board must disqualify himself from participating in consideration of the (rezoning) application . . ."

officials should have less to fear in terms of a damaging suit against them; they should have less concern for a financial loss resulting from acts performed in their official capacity than if this doctrine were not available. To illustrate the protection sovereign immunity provides, a suit, similar to *Fleming v. Albemarle*, filed in Loudoun Count was argued from the standpoint of legislative officials being immune under the doctrine of sovereign immunity.[109] The Circuit supervisors are covered by sovereign immunity against suits for tortious acts committed while they are acting within the sphere of actual legislative activity. Knowledge of these provisions which appear to help minimize the impact of personal liability lawsuits against public officials in Virginia may have contributed to and influenced their responses to a recent Virginia Municipal League survey and to the questionnaire which accompanies this study.

During 1977, the Virginia Municipal League "conducted a study of the offices of mayor and council members in Virginia cities and towns" and found that, while "there is still a dedicated pool of citizens willing to serve in (a public capacity), there is an apparent disinclination on the part of a growing number of citizens to step forward for the cause of municipal government."[110] The results of the study show that "the erosion of power from the local level to state and federal governments, which has occurred

109. *Andrew I. Dobranski, et al. v. Board of Supervisors of Loudoun County, et al.*, Chancery No. 5575, Circuit Court of Loudoun County. (Decree entered May 26, 1977, Penn, J.).Complainants had alleged that the Board of Supervisors conspired to delay and deny rezoning applica tions made to it and thereby cause damage to them. The damages sought were the alleged additional sum the subject property would be worth if complainants had received their request.
The County argued from the landmark case of *Tenny v. Brandhove*, 341 u.s. 367 (1951)which accorded absolute immunity to state legislators acting within the sphere of their legislative activity that a county as a political subdivision of the state enjoys the same sovereign immunity as the state.
Municipal officials are also granted immunity under the doctrine when the municipality is responsible for a governmental function and the official is acting in a legislative capacity. *Shannon v. Hicks*, 434 F. Supp. 803 (1977); *McCray v. City of Lake Louisville*, 332 S.W. 2d 837 (Ky. Ct. App. 1960 ; *Masters v. Hart*, 189 Va. 969 (1949).

110. Michael S. Deeb, "The Eclipse of Local Government: A Time of Concern," *Virginia Town and City*, Vol. 13, No. 1 (January 1978), 4.

during this century, is a principal cause of the (elected city officials' frustration)."[111] Survey, the VML study results show, among other concerns, that elected officials are "confused and frustrated with the increasingly complex nature of municipal government, while at the same time not having pertinent up to date training and information to assist them in making decisions."[112]

Although the VML Study documents many concerns that "irritate mayors and councilmen about their jobs," the threat of personal liability suits is not among the "frustrations."[113] While this threat is not mentioned, it is conceivable that a certain degree of "frustration" could contribute inadvertently to acts which may result in a personal liability suit against any one or more elected officials. To get a feel for the perceived threat of personal liability the questionnaire accompanying this research in Appendix A was designed and presented *to* several elected and appointed officials *to* elicit their responses to fifteen questions related to personal liability suits.[114] The questionnaire was circulated among the officials in four Virginia localities: one city and three counties, each with an estimated population exceeding fifty thousand. The responses to the questionnaire indicate that generally public officials should be held accountable for their acts, even to the extent "being accountable" means having a liability suit filed against them for negligence in acts done in their official capacities. All officials (100 percent) who responded to the survey either agree or strongly agree that public officials should be held accountable for their acts. Fifty-eight percent agreed that local officials who act negligently in their official capacities should stand trial for civil acts. The responses to the statement "personal liability lawsuits against public officials should be allowed" was evenly divided: Only fifty percent agreed that liability suits should be[115] allowed. Although seventy-five per-

111. Ibid., S–7.

112. Ibid., 6.

113. Ibid., Table 1, 5.

114. The survey was conducted during July-August, 1978. Twelve Public officials responded to the questionnaire.

115. Many of the respondents qualified their answers to this statement.

cent of the public officials who responded to the survey indicated that personal liability suits could have a negative effect on their willingness to accept (or remain in) a public office, another 75 percent either agreed or strongly agreed that personal liability is a risk which one voluntarily assumes by accepting a public position. The findings produced by the questionnaire may be inconclusive to some extent.[116] Nonetheless, the findings, together with the Virginia Municipal League and the National League of Cities studies, produce ample information to draw a conclusion that most public officials would not leave public office for the single reason that a personal liability lawsuit against them in their official capacities may be imminent; that there are other adverse situations which in conjunction with a potential lawsuit may, however, cause them to do so. In other words, most public officials will continue to serve as long as they recognize an overall community-wide benefit and a degree of personal gratification as a result of their service.

Although disagreeing with the statement in general, one official agreed that an official who willfully breaks the law should be personally liable. Another made essentially the same comment after noting the distinction between official liability and personal liability. This official agreed that an official should be publicly (officially) liable, i.e. the government pays rather than the individual official, if sued for performing a function in the name of the office. and under the authority of the office; on the other hand, the official should be personally liable for acts performed outside the authority of the office he/she occupies.

116. The officials have given different responses to the statements in the questionnaire if they had not been given some protection against liability suits. Eighty-three percent agreed that their governments provided some form of indemnification (or insurance) for officials or employees.

V

Policy Recommendations
for Legislative Action

HOLDING PUBLIC OFFICIALS PERSONALLY liable for their acts is an attempt on the part of the courts, legislature, and concerned citizens to make the officials more responsible and accountable in their official activities. It appears that the trend will continue relative to the number of public officials found to have violated the civil rights of individuals under civil and federal (Section 1983) laws. The public official may find it difficult to avoid lawsuits where municipalities or counties are declared immune by the rulings of the state courts, but certain measures and precautions may be taken by public officials to avoid being held liable for violation of an individual's rights. On the other hand, public officials who wish to avoid entirely the risk of being held personally liable may resign or not seek reelection.

As can be seen from the several cases and examples illustrated, legislative and judicial actions in response to the notion of personal liability vary from state to state. The question is to what extent should a public official be held liable. An answer to the first question depends on the action taken on the second question, that is, should immunity be provided the locality? In other words, should the Virginia legislature abrogate or limit sovereign immunity in Virginia to remove the threat of personal liability against the public official?

There is little or no question that theoretically a public official who negligently and with malicious intent· injures another should be liable for the action.[1] Whether the official is, in fact, liable will depend on a finding of "malicious" intent. Questions involving the state of mind of a particular individual are difficult to determine. Federal law generally provides immunity for discretionary acts, "even when they are accompanied by malicious motives."[2] Generally, under state law officials who act outside the scope of their authority are personally liable.[3]

It may be argued that legislative action by the Virginia legislation is not necessary to protect local governments and their officials from the harmful effects of liability suits. Currently Virginia's adherence to the doctrine of sovereign immunity relieves officials of some of the "chilling effects of suits on (them)."[4]But one observer notes: However,

> (from) the viewpoint of the citizen believing himself to be injured by a state or local official, it is very important that avenues of redress are open to him. If the state or locality cannot be sued at all, or cannot be sued for the type of damage in question, the citizen may have no recourse but to sue the official personally. Where the municipality or state can be sued, it will *generally* be in the interest of the aggrieved citizen to sue the state or local government because greater assets than its officials.[5]

Although the United States Supreme Court once held that local governments were completely immune from suit under the Civil Rights Act of 1871, now codified as 42 U.S.C., Section 1983,[6]

1. Brown, *Personal Liability of Public Officials*, 13.

2. Ibid., 1.

3. Ibid.

4. Ibid.

5. Ibid., 7.

6. *Monroe v. Pape*, 365 U.S. 167 (1967) cited in Howard W. Dobbins, "Municipalities Held Liable for Unconstitutional Actions," Virginia Town and City,

it has ruled recently that local governments may be sued as a person.[7] In this connection, it appears that insofar as the suits invoke federal jurisdiction, no action by the Virginia legislature to relieve the threat of official liability is necessary.

In review of *Monell*, it may be found that the Supreme Court decision benefits public officials who may fear reprisal brought by aggrieved or injured persons. On the other hand, however, that benefit may be offset by the burden of liability that local governments must bear in the wake of this ruling. An aggrieved individual bringing a suit for damages may now, suddenly, have a greater incentive to bring suit against the government than he would in bringing· a suit against an official; the aggrieved is likely to believe that the claim filed against the government will have a greater impact on the government and/or that a larger sum for damages will be awarded than if filed against the public official.

In Virginia, municipalities are immune from suits involving governmental or regulatory functions, so that the burden of liability in such governmental or regulatory matters as zoning, code enforcement and inspections is on the public official responsible. This conclusion is based upon the opinion of Chief Justice Hudgins in *Masters v. Hart*, 189 Va. 969 (1949) in which he stated:

> The City of Harrisonburg is a municipal corporation, and is charged with both governmental and proprietary duties. It is not liable for the negligence of its officers, servants or agents, when through them it is performing a purely governmental function for the benefit of the public. It is only where a municipality acts in a private, proprietary or ministerial capacity that it is liable in a tort action.[8]

In regard to legislative and court actions in other states, federal law and the United States Supreme Court rulings, and court decisions in the Virginia courts system, this study recommends and suggests that the Virginia legislature enact legislation which

---

Volume 13, (August 1978), 14.

7. *Monell v. Department City of New York*, decided, 1978 (46 LW 4569).

8. *Masters v. Hart*, 189 Va. 769 (1949).

defines the suits which may be brought against the local governments and set limits for the amount of award which may be offered individuals in bringing a suit against them. This legislation may be in the form of a tort claims act which also specifies the actions for which public officials will be personally liable under State law.

Several precautions may be taken by local governments and the individual public officials to avoid personal liability suits. The locality should pin-point potential areas of liability; put policies and rules in writing; consult legal counsel before adopting policies; and handle problems expeditiously. The officials should become familiar with the requirements of state and federal law; be knowledgeable of current and past policies of the respective local government; adopt a code of ethics for officials and employees; be open and honest with citizens and other officers and employees with regard to reasons for policies; and be fair and just.[9]

These suggested actions taken by the various governments and officials as may be appropriate, should help relieve the burden of liability for acts by both the governments and officials of suits which may arise. Due to the complexity of modern local government, an occasional liability suit is inevitable. However, by the observance and implementation of these recommendations, the number of successful suits filed should be reduced.

9. These suggestions are drawn from a variety of sources, including Neil R. Shortlidge, "Personal Liability of Local Public Officials Part III and IV," 245.

Conclusion

WHILE IT IS SUSPECTED that personal liability suits are increasing, "no systematically organized data exist on the frequency of personal liability suits against public officials."[1] This research effort, like some other studies, does not find that there is a surge of successful suits in which public officials have paid damages out of their own pockets.[2] It is found, however, that litigation against local officials charging violation of individual and civil rights is becoming more and more common, but few of these cases go to judgment favorable to the plaintiff.[3] This research does not find, therefore, support for beliefs that the threat of personal liability suits will influence public officials to leave public office or, otherwise, be unwilling to serve in a public capacity solely as a result of the rise in personal liability suits.

The rise in personal liability suits is attributed to a "suit conscious" society and to the complexity and growth of local governments; both of which complicate the public official's decision-making ability. Individuals, including those injured by a particular governmental policy or an official's decision, are not accepting grievous actions which go against their individual interests. Many are not content with exhausting administrative remedies; rather, they are turning to the courts for a remedy. Some portion of the

1. Brown, *Personal Liability of Public Officials*, 5.
2. See Roos, Public Official Liability: 1976," 1–6.
3. Liability of Council Members for Violation, 4.

rise in liability suits may be attributed to the expansion of local government. Local governments are growing more complex daily with the multitude of services and functions they are required to provide. In addition to their local functions, local units of government are mandated and, sometimes by necessity—through acceptance of intergovernmental transfers, obligated to perform functions which are, in effect, functions of the state or federal governments. These functions often conflict with the intent of the policies of one or all three levels of government, eliminate local options and discretionary actions and, in many instances set the stage for litigation. Of course, some of the litigation is brought about by an official's negligence, either through inability to keep abreast of developments affecting his/her decisions or through failure to act in a lawful manner. Since the government and its officials operate in a more open environment than they did in the past, primarily as a result of legislation providing for open meetings and more accessible public information, public officials must be more cautious and more aware of the decisions they make. Although a conscious effort on the part of the public official to avoid personal liability suits will help reduce the number of suits filed against them or the government, some preventive measures must be taken to avoid the possibility of successful liability lawsuits. Most states have addressed the problem of liability suits through judicial and legislative efforts. Liability insurance, legal representation and indemnification are available to many local governments. Although adherence to the doctrine of sovereign immunity by state governments has been a hedge against the chilling effects of liability suits, many states have recently abrogated sovereign immunity and adopted tort claims legislation.

Virginia currently adheres to the doctrine of sovereign immunity. Also, legislation is available which provides that local governments may purchase liability insurance for its officials and employees. Local governments may also provide legal counsel to represent officials and employees and indemnify local officials who have incurred costs as a result of a liability suit filed against them in their official and lawful capacities.

It is observed through this study, however, that there is a trend throughout state governments to abrogate or limit sovereign immunity. Although such legislation benefits the individual public official by removing some of the threat of personal loss as a result of his govern mental-related activities, the abrogation of this age-old doctrine opens the way for more damaging and costly suits against the government than would ordinarily be filed against the public official; aggrieved individuals may see an added incentive in filing a claim against the government than against the individual official in expectation of a larger sum being awarded for damages.

If what some state courts have done by judicially abrogating sovereign immunity is any indication of what may happen in Virginia, the Virginia legislature would be well-advised to enact a tort claims act. This act would legislatively abrogate or limit sovereign immunity, define the suits under which the government would be liable, specify the acts for which the public official and governmental employees would be personally liable, and set the limits on the size of the award which may be offered for damages suffered by plaintiffs. In 1978, the Virginia legislature reviewed a "draft" tort claims act presented to it by a legislative subcommittee. Although the draft document left some questions unanswered, it included several provisions which would aid both local governments and officials in coping with liability suits. It is recommended that the legislature rethink this proposal and give serious consideration to adopting it.

While actions taken at the State level are important in addressing the problem of liability suits in Virginia's local governments, the problem will not be solved alone by one level or branch of government; all are involved and have a role in reducing the burden of personal liability on the public official. The public official, of course, is not relieved from his personal responsibility in this effort. A conscious, individual effort to reduce liability suits through responsible public decisions will help hold the number of successful suits to a minimum.

Appendix

The following questionnaire was used to solicit responses to questions and. issues related to personal liability of public officials in Virginia. The responses of selected officials have been recorded and are presented next to the question in percentages of officials responding. All officials responded to each question.

QUESTIONNAIRE
PERSONAL LIABILITY/WILLINGNESS TO SERVE

To: Local Legislators and Chief Executives
(Note: If you wish to comment on any of the following statements, please write on the back of the questionnaire.)

Statement/Question	Strongly Agree	Agree	Undecided	Disagree	Strongly Disagree	% Responses
1.Personal liability lawsuits against public officials should be allowed.	(1) 8%	(5) 42%		(4) 33%	(2) 17%	100

Statement/ Question	Strongly Agree	Agree	Undecided	Disagree	Strongly Disagree	% Responses
2.Persons injured by a public official's decision should be compensated.	(1) 8%	(6) 50%		(2) 17%	(3) 25%	100
3. Public officials should be held ac countable for their acts.	(5) 42%	(7) 58%				100
4. The social objective of the concept of personal liability is 100 to provide a channel through which an injured party may be compensated.	(2) 17%	(6) 50%	(1) 8%	(3) 25%		100
5. Public officials should be immune for their acts committed under the law, even if by doing the act it results in a violation of an individual's rights.	(3) 25%	(7) 58%		(2) 17%		100
6. Local legislators who act negligently in their official capacities should stand trial for civil acts.	(3) 25%	(4) 33%	(1) 8%		(4) 33%	100
7. Public officials should be held ac countable for their acts.	(5) 42%	(7) 58%				100

Statement/Question	Strongly Agree	Agree	Undecided	Disagree	Strongly Disagree	% Responses
8. The social objective of the concept of personal liability is to provide a channel through which an injured party may be compensated.	(2) 17%	(6) 50%	(1) 8%	(3) 25%		100
9. Public officials should be immune for their acts committed under the law, even if by doing the act it results in a violation of an individual's rights.	(3) 25%	(7) 58%		(2) 17%		100
10. Local legislators who act negligently in their official capacities should stand trial for civil acts.	(3) 25%	(4) 33%	(1) 8%		(4) 33%	100
11. In making their decision, local legislators consider the likelihood of a personal liability lawsuit against them.	(1) 8%	(3) 25%	(1) 8%	(6) 50%	(1) 8%	100
12. In administrative matters, e.g., approving a developer's site plan, local legislators should be personally liable for damages.			(2) 17%	(6) 50%	(4) 33%	100

Statement/ Question	Strongly Agree	Agree	Undecided	Disagree	Strongly Disagree	% Responses
13. A local legislator who acts criminally negligent in his/her official capacity should stand trial.	(5) 42%	(7) 58%				100
14. City/county managers/ executives should be personally liable for their decisions.	(3) 25%	(3) 25%		(6) 50%		100
15. If personal liability suits against public officials continue, they will be less willing to accept public office.	(2) 17%	(7) 58%	(3) 25%			100
16. Being "personally liable" for your acts affects your willing ness to continue to serve in a public capacity.	(7) 58%				(5) 42%	100
17. Local legislators assume a potential personal liability when they accept public office.	(9) 75%				(3) 25%	100
18. Does your government insure its officials against personal liability suits?	(7) 58%				(5) 42%	100

Statement/ Question	Strongly Agree	Agree	Undecided	Disagree	Strongly Disagree	% Responses
19. Does your government provide any form of indemnification to its officials or employees?	(1) 83%				(2) 17%	100

Bibliography

Books, Periodicals, and Unpublished Material

"A Proposed Reciprocal Insurance Company for the Virginia Municipal League." Virginia Town and City, Vol. 14, No. 4, 1979, 6–7.

Advisory Commission on Intergovernmental Relations. "States Tackle Tough Fiscal Issues," Intergovernmental Perspective, Vol. 5, No. 1, 1979, 6–30.

Aronson, J. Richard and Schwartz, Eli, Editors. Management Policies in Local Government Finance. Washington, DC: International1975.

Barnard, Chester I. "The Functions of the Executive." Cambridge, Massachusetts: Harvard University Press, 1968.

Black, Henry Campbell. Black's Law Dictionary. St. Paul, Minnesota: West Publishing Company, 1968.

Brown, Peter G. Personal Liability of Public Officials, "Sovereign Immunity and Compensation for Loss." Columbus, Ohio: Academy For Contemporary Publishers, 1977.

Camden, Howard B., and Richard J. Heskin, "A Look at the Crisis in Municipal Insurance." Michigan Municipal Review, 1977, 126, 128, 135–36.

Christian,· Gary. "Minimize Losses and Cut Premiums." Alabama Municipal Journal, 1975, 6–7, 24.

Committee on the Office of Attorneys General. Sovereign Immunity: The Liability of Government and its Public Officials. Raleigh, North Carolina: National Association of Attorneys General, 1976.

Commonwealth of Virginia. "Initial Staff Study for Joint Subcommittee Studying Insurance Problems of Localities." Virginia Division of Legislative Services, 1978.

Commonwealth of Virginia. "Report of the Senate and House Committees for Courts of Justice." On Governmental Immunity to the Governor and the General Assembly of Virginia. House Document 92. Session, 1975.

Bibliography

Cowan, Jim Magee. "An Analysis of the Evolving Theory of Personal Liability of Educational Trustees for Their Official Acts." Ed. D. Dissertation, University of Houston, 1977.

Davis, Kenneth C. "Administrative Law: Cases, Texts, Problems." St. Paul, Minnesota: West, 1973.

Davis, Kenneth C. "Administrative Law of the Seventies: Supplement Law Treatises." St. Paul, Minnesota: West, 1976.

Davis, Kenneth C. "Administrative Law Treatises." 2nd ed. San Diego, California: K. C. Davis, 1978.

Deeb, Michael S. "The Eclipse of Local Government: A Time of Concern". Virginia Municipal League, Vol. 13, No. 1, 1978, 4–6.

Dobbins, Howard W. "Liability Insurance for Governmental Officers and Employees." Virginia Town and City. Vol. 11, No. 8, 1976, 11–12.

"Fleming Petitions Allowed," Daily Progress, June 15, 1978.

Harmes, Bradley K. Memorandum On Insurance Seminar. Richmond: Virginia Municipal League, 1978.

Henning, Kenneth. "Liability of City Officials." Texas, Town and City, 1975, 4–5, 7–8.

Henning, Kenneth K. "Public Official Liability: A Trending Toward 'Administrative Malpractices.'" Management Information Service Report 8. Washington, DC: International City Management Association, 1976, 1–9.

International City Management Association. The Municipal Yearbook. Washington, DC: International City Management Association, 1977.

Jaffe, Louis L. "Suits Against Governments and Officers: Damage Actions." Harvard Law Review, Vol. 77, 1963, 209–23.

Jaffe, Louis L. "Suits Against Governments and Officers: Sovereign Immunity." Harvard Law Review, Vol. 77, 1963, 1–39.

Jones, George E. "The Accountable Society: Are Lawyers, Courts, Big Government Dulling America's Moral Sense?" U.S. News and World Report, September 26, 1977 84–85.

"Liability of Council Members for Violation of Civil Rights." Illinois Municipal Review, 1976, 4.

"Liability Insurance for Florida Cities." Florida Municipal Record, 1977, 2–9.

Management and Control of Growth. Edited by Randall W. Scott, David J. Brower, and Dallas D. Miner. Washington, DC: The Urban Land Institute, 1975.

Mashaw, Jerry L., and Richard A. Merrill. "The American Public Law System." St. Paul, Minnesota: West Publishing Company, 1975.

McManis, Charles R. "Personal Liability of State Officials." State Government, Vol. 49, 1976, 86–90.

Michie Company, Michie's Jurisprudence. Charlottesville, Virginia: The Michie Company, 1951–1978.

Morgan, David R. "Oklahoma Enacts Changes in Municipal Tort Liability," National Civic Review, 1978, 324.

Bibliography

Mosher, Frederick C. "Watergate: Implications for Responsible Government." New York: Basic, 1974.

Murray, James B. Esquire. Appendix for Appellant's Briefs—Citizen's County Taxpayers, Inc. v. James N. Fleming, et al. No. 76-230 (4th Cr. 1977).

Murray, James B., Jr. Briefs For Appellants—Citizens for Albemarle, Inc., and Albemarle County Taxpayers, Inc. v. James N. Fleming, et al. Record No. 6-2308 (4th Cr. 1977).

Neher, Estelle (Miss). Clerk. Albemarle County Board of Supervisors. Minutes of the Board and Exhibits Pertaining to the Rezoning Application of James N. Fleming, et al. Albemarle County, Virginia, 1978.

Nigro, Felix A. "Modern Public Administration." 2nd ed. New York: Harper and Row, 1970.

Parker, Thomas D., Insurance Administrator, Arlington County. Letter to Hugh Fisher, Virginia Division of Legislative Services, Arlington County, Virginia. May 8, 1978.

Payne, Frederick. Liability Insurance File Self-insurance. Charlottesville, Va.: George R. St. John Associates, Attorneys At Law, 1977.

Peet, William. *A Nationwide Problem: Putting Perspective on the Risks of Liability for Public Officials, and For Everybody Else.* League of Minnesota Cities, 1976.

"Pennsylvania Municipal Liability", Pennsylvania Township News, 1977, 9-11.

Peterson, Nancy Mitchell. "Holding Public Office—A Risky Business," Nation's Cities, Vol. 14, No. 8. 1976, 19, 22, 24, 38.

Poindexter, Gerald G. Brief for Appellees—Citizens for Albermarle, Inc. and Albermarle County Taxpayers, inc., v. James N. Fleming, et al. No. 76-2308 (4th Cir. 1977).

Prosser, William L. *The Law of Torts.* St. Paul, Minnesota: West Publishing Company, 1971.

"Recent Decisions." *Civil Rights: Corporate Directors Held Personally Liable for Intentional Racial Discrimination Despite Due Diligence to Know the Law.* University of Richmond Law Review, Vol. 10 (1975), 197.

Shepard's Virginia Citations. Colorado Springs, Co.: Shepard's Citations, Inc.

Shortlidge, Neil R. *Personal Liability of Local Public Officials and the Official Immunity Doctrine, Part III and IV.* Kansas Government Journal, Vol. 63, 1977, 241-45.

Spahn, Gary J., and David E. Boone. "Private Discrimination Actions Filed in Federal Court: Non-substantive Matters Affecting Liability and Relief." University of Richmond Law Review, Vol. 12, 1977, 88-134.

St. John, George R. Letter to William Broaddus, Esq. RE: Self-Insurance Program #ACC-77-352. Charlottesville, Va.: George R. St. John, Associates, Attorneys At Law, June 23, 1977.

"Surprising Trend: You Can Beat City Hall." U.S. News and World Report, 1977, 67-68.

"The Municipal Liability Insurance Crisis—An Overview." Western City 1976, 6, 36.

Bibliography

"The Municipal Liability Situation." Insurance Facts from Insurance Information Institute, San Francisco, California: 1976.

"The New World of Municipal Liability." Washington, DC: National League of Cities, 1978.

"Torts." Virginia Law Review, Vol. 89 1973, 1590–1620.

Treakle, James E. Jr., Letter to George R. St. John, Esq. RE: Potential Conflict of Interest: Application of James N. Fleming. Charlottesville, Va.: Office of the Commonwealth's Attorney—Albemarle County, March 8, 1978.

Virginia Association of Counties. Directory of Virginia County Officials. Charlottesville, Virginia: Virginia Association of Counties, 1974.

Virginia Code Annotated. Charlottesville, Virginia: The Michie Company, Law Publishers.

Virginia Municipal League. Virginia Governmental Officials. Richmond, Virginia: The Virginia Municipal League, 1971.

"Virginia Reports." Charlottesville, Virginia: The Michie Company. Warp, George A. "Municipal Tort Liability In Virginia," *Report of the Bureau of Public Administration* Series B, No. 8. University, Virginia: Division of Publications of the Bureau of Public Administration, 1941.

Warp, George A. *Recent Statutory Developments in Municipal Liability in Tort* (1936). 2 Leg. Notes On Loc. Govt. 89, 100.

Wilson, James Q. "Political Organizations." New York: Basic Books: 1973.

Wisconsin Legislative Council. State Capitol, Madison, Wisconsin. *Legislation Relating to Public Liability of Local Governments*. Report No. 9 To The 1977 Legislature. March 25, 1977.

Interviews

Agnor, Guy B., County Executive—Albemarle County, Virginia. Interview. July 14, 1978.

Apperson, J. Ruffin, Member—Chesterfield County Board of Supervisors, Chesterfield, Virginia. Interview, July 18, 1979.

Dorrier, Lindsay G., Jr., Member—Albemarle County Board of Supervisors, Charlottesville, Virginia. Interview, July 21, 1978.

Faison, Frank A., County Manager-Henrico County, Virginia. Interview, July 17, 1978.

Fisher, Gerald E., Chairman, Albemarle County Board of Supervisors, Charlottesville, Virginia. Interview, July 24, 1978.

Girone, Joan (Mrs.), Member—Chesterfield County Board of Supervisors, Chesterfield, Virginia. Interview, July 18, 1978.

Jinkins, George W., Jr., Chairman, Henrico County Board of Supervisors, Henrico County, Virginia. Interview, August 4, 1978.

Kenney, Walter T., Member—Richmond City Council, Richmond, Virginia. Interview, August 4, 1978.

Bibliography

Liedinger, William. City Manager, City of Richmond, Virginia. Interview, July 20, 1978.

Meiser, Nicholas M., County Administrator—Chesterfield County, Virginia. Interview, July 18, 1978.

Murray, James B., Richmond and Fishburne Attorneys at Law. Charlottesville, Virginia. Interviews, March 15, 1978; June 30, 1978.

Rennie, Wayland W., Member—Richmond City Council, Richmond, Virginia. Interview, August 18, 1978.

Rilee, Eugene T., Jr., Member—Henrico County Board of Supervisors, Henrico County, Virginia. Interview, August 17, 1978.

Serow, William J., Research Director, Tayloe Murphy Institute—University of Virginia. Interview, April 4, 1978.

Treakle, James E., Jr., Assistant Commonwealth Attorney—Albemarle County. Charlottesville, Virginia. Interview, March 15, 1978.

Winbushe, William, Assistant (Richmond) City Attorney, Richmond, Virginia. Interview, March 14, 1978.